WHAT IT TAKES TO BE YOURSELF

WHAT IT TAKES TO BE YOURSELF

From Seeking Success
to Embodying Purpose
through Compassion

PINUCCIA CONTINO

Arkadinia

Copyright © 2026 Pinuccia Contino

Published by Arkadinia

All rights reserved.

Cover artwork: *Constructions* (1961), Anne Luc. Oil on canvas. Private collection. Used with permission.

No part of this book may be reproduced or transmitted in any form or by any electronic or mechanical means, including storage and retrieval systems, without permission in writing from the author or the publisher, except for brief quotations in reviews.

Legal deposit: Belgium (KBR – Royal Library of Belgium)

ISBN (Print): 978-2-9604105-0-1

ISBN (e-book): 978-2-9604105-1-8

This book is, among other things, a memoir. It reflects the author's present recollection of her experiences over time. Most names and identifying details have been changed, some events condensed, and dialogue reconstructed.

The information and views in this book are solely those of the author and do not reflect any official opinion of her employer. Reference to the latter is made only when necessary to understand the author's personal experiences and perceptions.

While every effort has been made to ensure accuracy at the time of publication, the author and publisher assume no responsibility for any loss, damage, or disruption caused by errors or omissions.

This publication is sold with the understanding that the publisher is not providing professional services. Readers seeking expert advice should consult a qualified professional.

References to organizations or websites are provided for informational purposes only and do not constitute endorsement. Websites mentioned in this work may have changed or disappeared since the time of writing.

For Serge

*I do believe it is possible to create,
even without ever writing a word or painting a picture,
by simply molding one's inner life.
And that, too, is a deed.*
—Etty Hillesum, *An Interrupted Life*

Contents

Foreword	i
Introduction	1
Prologue: Success, What's in a Name?	5

PART I: COMING FROM FAR, FAR AWAY

Chapter One: To Be or not to Be Wonder Woman	21
Chapter Two: When Unconditional Love Gets in the Way	43
Chapter Three: From Sicily to Belgium with Purpose	67

PART II: FINDING SELF-FULFILLMENT AT WORK

Chapter Four: Humility, the Underrated Power	95
Chapter Five: Vulnerability, the Unassuming Strength	117
Chapter Six: Pride and Forgiveness	143
Chapter Seven: About Violence and Limiting Beliefs	167
Chapter Eight: What Death Has to Do with Compassionate Leadership	195

PART III: SURRENDERING TO LIFE PURPOSE— AND THRIVING

Chapter Nine: Dropping the Magic Mirror to Face Shame	219
Chapter Ten: Approaching Money through the Lens of Triggers	245
Chapter Eleven: Getting to Joy	267

Chapter Twelve: Aligning with Purpose through Compassion	287
Did You Say "Conclusion"?	305
Acknowledgements (my way)	309
Recommended Resources (my way too)	311

Foreword

When I first met Pinuccia Contino in 2021, she arrived in the Applied Compassion Training (ACT) program with a fierce intellect, a sincere spiritual curiosity, and a kind of grounded determination that I have come to associate with people on the cusp of real transformation. Even then, there was a question quietly taking shape in her: What does it mean to live a life that is truly one's own? Not a life shaped by expectation, achievement, recognition, or inherited notions of success—but a life aligned with purpose, authenticity, and compassion.

Over the years since, I have had the privilege of witnessing her evolve from someone striving to meet the world's external demands into someone listening—deeply—to the truth of her own heart. I still remember a conversation we had in 2022, when she asked whether writing a book about compassion in her life made sense. I told her that even if she wrote it only for herself, the process would illuminate her journey in ways she couldn't yet imagine. What I did not know at the time was how fully she would devote herself to that task, or how beautifully she would weave together reflection, vulnerability, and wisdom in these pages.

This book is not a linear memoir, nor is it simply a collection of insights. It is something more intimate: a map of one woman's lived experience of becoming. Through childhood joys and sorrows, professional triumphs and disappointments, losses, reckonings, and profound moments of awakening, she invites readers into an exploration of what it takes to shed the layers that obscure our truest self. With clarity and courage, she names the forces we all wrestle with—ambition, image, power, perfectionism, money—and shows how each can become a doorway to compassion when met with honesty rather than judgment.

What moves me most about this work is that she did not write it for personal catharsis alone. She wrote it because she wanted it to serve. She wrote because she hoped that her hard-earned lessons might ease someone else's path or help another person pause and ask: What if authenticity is not something to achieve, but something to remember? That intention—to be of benefit—permeates every chapter.

Readers will find here not only storytelling, but tools: self-inquiry prompts, metaphors, reflections, and practices shaped by her studies at Stanford's Center for Compassion and Altruism Research and Education (CCARE), which were woven into the ACT program. Although ACT has since concluded, a new successor course—The CCARE Compassion Lab (CCL)—is now emerging. It carries forward the same spirit that animates this book: that compassion is not a soft ideal, but a powerful and 'transformative force' that reveals purpose, restores agency, and makes authentic living possible.

My hope is that as you travel with Pinuccia through these pages, you allow her insights and her courage to stir something in you. This memoir is an invitation—to slow down, to question inherited definitions of success, to honor your own wounds with tenderness, and to consider that your deepest purpose may already be whispering to you, waiting to be heard.

It has been a privilege to witness her journey. I applaud you as you embark on your own.

—Robert Cusick
Director of Compassion Education
Center for Compassion and Altruism Research and Education
(CCARE)
Stanford University

Introduction

Courage to change, Sia

I am so thrilled to meet you, dear reader! Thank you for choosing to read this book. Before you dive into it, here are a few keys to help you unlock the doors to the spaces you will explore in the following pages.

First of all, this is both a memoir and a self-help book. The memoir weaves together episodes and threads of my life that underpin my transformational journey toward authenticity. It highlights how I have gradually become more myself, expanding and transcending the mainstream concept of success to discover, befriend, and embrace my life purpose. And how every step I have taken toward aligning my authentic being with my purpose has increased my happiness.

Putting on paper the episodes of my life that might be of service to you in pursuing your unique path toward self-fulfillment is the reason why I decided to write this memoir in the first place. Writing this book has been quite a long and wondrous adventure for me, and I could only complete it because I was always supported, energized, and motivated by the hope that it might help you too to become freer and happier. It was not an easy walk, to say the least. But I am truly grateful finally to be able to offer my personal "success" story as an invitation to you to explore your own through the lens of common humanity.

Along this path, I have become aware of a universal enabler of authenticity and purpose: compassion, our drive to decrease suffering in us and others. Every life is unique, yet everybody suffers. Suffering has no preference and does not spare any human being, whatever their circumstances may be. We all have the power to make our life miserable, even when others believe we have everything to be happy. But that's not the end of the story. My life experience—together with the science of compassion—has made me aware that when our suffering is met with compassion, including toward ourselves, we nourish our life purpose and clear the path leading to who we truly are.

Against this background, every chapter will depict some of my life experiences from a specific angle as a starting point to share self-inquiry questions, instruments, and practices that may offer you ways and insights to (re)define your own unique path to happiness according to your personal circumstances. At the end of each chapter you will find a box gathering all the self-inquiry questions that inspired or just appeared in that chapter, to assist your personal practice. You will also be able to write your own questions inside the box and turn your copy of this book into your own unique version of it. Finally, for each chapter I will recommend a relevant resource (a video, an article, a meditation, a quote, or a project) that I consider particularly powerful.

The book plays with experience and co-creation in ways that will hopefully inspire you. For example, I have chosen a different color for every chapter (in the e-book version). Moreover, each chapter opens with the title of a song that I find very much aligned with its content. I suggest that you listen to it (and read its lyrics, if any) before you start reading, just to get into the chapter's overall mood and unveil some clues. So, by way of introduction, if you haven't done so yet, you may want to go back to the top of page 1 and listen to the song I chose as a cue for the entire book. At the end, you will find the link to download the entire book playlist as a lasting gift from me. And I will invite you to enrich it, or to build an alternative one, if you so wish.

Last but not least, at the end of the book I have organized the resources I recommend in a quite unusual, and hopefully useful, way. Feel free to explore them at any point. You may also want to add your own resources to the list—I have made space for that.

I would like to end on a personal wish: when you are finished, would you mind reaching out to me on LinkedIn (here: https://www.linkedin.com/in/pinuccia-contino/) and sharing how all this has landed with you, and whether you found it a bit helpful? My plan is to develop a readers' community in a collaborative way. I will offer you the opportunity to post the stories, feedback, resources, and songs that you choose to share with me and with the community that I hope will gather around us. Because I believe that this is just the start of our interconnected journey.

PROLOGUE

Success, What's in a Name?

The Climb, Miley Cyrus

In May 2024, just back from a two-year soul-seeking trip around the world, one of my best friends and allies asked me a powerful question. I had asked her whether she would accept to read my manuscript, even if it was not final yet, because I valued her views enormously and I was sure her remarks would help me progress. She agreed.

After reading most of it, she asked me why I was writing this book.

The first time I replied very confidently that I was writing it to help people who, like me, think that success in terms of career, wealth and impact automatically brings self-fulfillment and happiness, while actually it's more complicated than that. I even ventured to describe the type of audience I was targeting, as if I were in front of a potential publisher. I felt quite excited and satisfied by what I thought was a very appropriate, thoughtful and well-founded reply.

She smiled and asked again, "Why are you really writing this book?"

I paused, a little puzzled by her reaction, and I dived deeper inside me. I then added that I had always loved writing, and even though for decades I could not find the time to write, I had finally found the motivation and perseverance needed. I thought this was due to the possibility that some of my life learnings could help others become happier.

She smiled again and repeated, "This is all fine, but why are you really writing this book?"

It felt a bit like in the "Groundhog Day" movie, I mean the unnerving situation repeating itself once, twice, three and more times, when the alarm clock goes off and Bill Murray has to start the same day with the same sequence of events all over again. This time, I had no more prompt replies in store. Realizing that I was struggling with the ultimate reason for my writing, with her usual kindness she came to my rescue and offered me her precious insight.

"I believe that deep down you are writing for yourself. I do not mean in the sense of being selfish, but in the sense of giving yourself the love that was denied to you in so many situations, all along your life. You are filling with self-love the gaps and the holes that the lack of love opened in your heart."

Tears came to my eyes. I realized that I had never heard a more beautiful description of self-compassion. I had studied compassion from a scientific angle during my Applied Compassion Training at Stanford University in 2021. So, I knew that self-compassion can be defined as being able to notice our suffering and doing something to decrease it, which basically means tending to ourselves when we suffer, just like our best friend would do. But she was revealing to me something I was not fully

What It Takes to Be Yourself

aware of: that I had become capable of practicing self-compassion as a habit, after studying and understanding it cognitively.

Let's stop here for a moment and let me check in with you: can you remember the last time you offered love to yourself because you were hurting? A time when you behaved like your best friend instead of criticizing yourself, calling yourself bad names, regretting that you had not replied in a better way, reacted more promptly, done or not done something?

And if you don't, can you think now of a situation where you were longing for care and attention because something was lacking inside? This might be the right moment to close your eyes and give yourself a hug that comes from the heart. And if not now, maybe you can try later.

I hope my little opening story has intrigued you enough to become curious about what has happened to me along the path toward what I used to consider success and now call life purpose. Maybe you are starting to wonder what self-compassion and love for self have to do with success. Be prepared: I have many more questions in store for you. When I was a child I was well known in the family for always asking questions, and I particularly liked to ask questions starting with "why". So when you come to my question points, in case you are feeling annoyed or irritated, just imagine that little Pinuccia aged six is asking you those questions.

Me aged six (my father's picture)

Even better, may I suggest you try to connect with yourself as a little child, and see what happens?

When I say "connect", I mean feeling your presence as a child in your heart—not thinking of yourself as a child. Feeling directly, without thinking the feeling, is not necessarily easy, and it may require some practice. In my experience, at the beginning it really helps to foster this connection by looking at a photo you like of yourself at a tender age, or listening to your recorded child's voice. Little by little, you may start feeling exactly the way you felt when you were that young: loving, playful, open,...

I personally experienced a very strong connection with myself as a child for the first time on March 8, 2022, and it was so powerful that I can still remember it in detail. Let me set the scene: that Tuesday evening I was in Brussels, the capital city of Belgium, where I have been living since 1991. I had spent a full, intense day at the office and had just come back home. That day had been no usual day: it was the first day back to work after months of restrictions due to the COVID-19 pandemic. Just for you to picture the setting if you are a visual person, at home I work from a very colorful room, which also became my favorite place to study, write, and meditate. That evening I closed the door of my home office, sat down—not on a meditation cushion, but on my Swiss ball to prevent back issues—and started meditating. For those who have never experienced it, meditation is a way to train our attention on one thing at a time. I closed my eyes after finding my balance and focused on the breath, slowly and calmly breathing in and breathing out. I could feel the air entering my nostrils without first thinking of it, a sensation I appreciate very much.

I had chosen a particular form of meditation, which is called "visualization". In a visualization, you follow or give yourself some prompts that help you picture a specific landscape or background, bring up identified actors or elements, and carry out a series of actions. All this may (or may not) let hints, memories and even epiphanies emerge from inside, through the path of intuition. So, that evening I started with visualizing myself as an elderly person, to get some insight from a wiser version of myself. I reached the place I imagined I could be living in when I would be 100 years old. It was a very warm, large, and cozy wooden chalet with a lovely terrace overlooking a lake surrounded by mountains. The place was wrapped in a friendly and quaint atmosphere, and the entire family—I could recognize my husband, our three kids, and their future families, including a few small kids—was present, celebrating my long and happy life.

I must admit I didn't look bad at all, in spite of my full century, the most noticeable difference with myself on that day, at nearly 55, being that my hair had gone completely white. Still, the curls and the hair length were similar, giving my older version a charm that age could not beat. We hugged, same as granddaughter and grannie, and yet I had no doubt it was myself—just at a different point of my life. After admiring the lake view and having a loving look at my children and future grandchildren (a few were running around), I asked my elder version whether we could go to a private room. Once inside a welcoming studio with wooden walls, she invited me to sit in a leather armchair in front of her. Then I asked her my first question.

"From now on, what is important for me to pay attention to?"

100-year-old Pinuccia looked into my eyes for a few moments, filling my heart with love and benevolence, and then said, "Heart-to-heart connection."

I let that revelation sink in, experiencing a surge of joy and energy in my body.

Then I asked a second question.

"What's not important, that I shouldn't worry about?"

There, the reply came like lightning.

"All the rest."

After a moment of astonishment, I started sensing where she was headed to. I knew myself a tad, after all. So I felt the urgency to ask a third question.

"What advice can you give me on how to live my life?"

My white-haired self smiled and replied, "Never say no."

I was flabbergasted: that was something I could certainly meditate upon forever! However, the visualization was not finished yet. Older Pinuccia got up (without difficulty, I gladly noticed) and handed me a beautiful wooden shrine. The artistic object contained a gift that my older self wanted me to be guided by.

I was not expecting my heartbeat to accelerate, but actually this is what happened when I opened the shrine and a hologram of my picture at six (the same one as above) emerged. Exactly like Princess Leia in the first "Star Wars" movie.

I started weeping, looking at the innocent face gently staring at me with the kindest of smiles. Suddenly, I felt that myself aged six, 55, and 100 was in the same place at the same time. It was as if time could not separate me from myself in the different periods of my life.

How could that be possible, let alone true? I had been looking for an answer all my life, since I was a pre-teen. I used to spend hours reflecting and journaling about a seemingly unsolvable problem: how could I be aware of who I was at any one point in time, while being in a constant flow of change? And still now, if I try to address this problem with my brain, I cannot find a way out. That visualization offered me another way to approach the question: not intellectually or cognitively, but experiencing feelings and emotions that brought me to its core and gave me profound insights. This experience helped me accept that I can feel who I am even if I cannot define what it means to be myself. The upside to this conundrum is that I can keep on exploring, and this can reveal facets, elements, and aspects of my being that I may not necessarily grasp intellectually—which does not mean they are less true. And the most surprising fact is that I can feel whole while being unable to describe every aspect of me.

At this point, I invite you to take a deep breath and pause. I know it's a lot to process. You can even close your eyes if it feels OK for you, and continue focusing on the breath. Breathing in, breathing out. Slowly, calmly. Feeling whole with your body. For as long as you please.

✳ ✳ ✳

Why am I sharing this very personal experience with you? As a first step, you can ask yourself the three powerful questions emerging from the visualization I described above even if you do not practice or do not fancy meditation.

Secondly, let me invite you to go deeper, and ask yourself: what makes me unmistakably me? This question is not limited to your self-perception—the way you feel you are who you are. You can develop this self-inquiry in all directions, for example:

- What makes me feel alive?
- What do I bring to the world?
- What is my North Star?

I invite you to take some time when you feel ready to journal, reflect, or meditate (whatever you prefer) on this. And maybe also ask yourself what happens when you become aware of something about yourself: what is the difference between before and after? Can you feel it? How would you describe or represent it?

If you try this out, you will actually find yourself testing and practicing self-awareness. Self-awareness is something I will be returning often to, as in my view it is an indispensable element of personal growth, and it is something available to everybody, provided you cultivate it. This is the reason why I started by sharing with you a couple of situations where my self-awareness increased, helping me become more rooted in who I am and offering me a compass that is still guiding me through good times and bad.

I do believe we human beings are all a work in progress. Some are further down the path, others are just starting, depending on our specific circumstances, which belong uniquely to each of us. To me, the beauty and the challenge of our common human condition merge when we realize that at no point can we say that we are complete, we have arrived, or there is no further possible growth. This happens exactly because wherever we happen to be on our life path, we can always expand further. In particular, through the lessons that suffering teaches us. Again, something that we all have in common: whoever has never suffered in their life, please say so. Nobody, right?

Of course, it would be extremely complex—and possibly arrogant of me—to try and address every angle of life to see what success means, entails, and requires. That's why I decided to approach this fundamental question, that practically everybody on earth asks themselves, from the work angle, including links with education and society. Romantic and family life will come into the picture only when necessary to better illustrate or convey my experiences and learnings from the professional sphere of my life.

Against this background, let's consider that for decades we have generally believed in a common definition of success. Success would primarily happen at work and involve a certain level of social recognition, power and influence on others, rank or career level, wealth, and standard of life. In spite of national and cultural differences, I have the impression that this general premise works quite well pretty much everywhere. If in your view it doesn't, feel free to adapt it to your reality. In any case, apart from the luckiest among us, most of the people I have met in my life seemed to be under the spell of some expectation (internalized, expressed by family, friends, at school/university, in their communities, ...) that they needed to adopt an external benchmark of success. The most famous of all is the American Dream, which has inspired and attracted also many people outside the US; but there are plenty of other similar success visions, like getting a job-for-life, continuing the family business, or fulfilling the parents' dreams of success. These, while being different, have all in common the fact that they are dictated from the outside.

The mainstream vision of success is something that my own life experience has amply debunked, and I will tell you how. However, this does not mean that I will be proposing to replace it with another recipe for success. At most, I will be offering questions for self-inquiry.

So, how does all this sound? Interesting, surprising, disturbing? Whatever your reaction may be, I get it. Therefore, let me share the long and winding road, as the Beatles would sing, that has led me to make wondrous discoveries about success and the meaning of life.

Now, I have conceived this entire book as a sort of experiment, comprising a memoir, a self-help book, and your own journey—if you wish to include it. Moreover, I am a huge fan of co-creation, and I hope you will pursue your own journey with me. That's why at the end of every chapter you will find a box that contains the questions I mention in that chapter, or that have been meaningful in shaping my understanding of the experiences I have highlighted. This way I hope you will get to explore your own, unique life experience, and distil your personal insights from it. Let's have a go at it!

To summarize and help you practice, through meditation, journaling, or self-reflection, I have listed here the self-inquiry questions underpinning the prologue:

- Can I take a deep breath now and feel my body?
- Can I bring to mind some moderate manifestations of suffering in my life? Have they brought any useful insight to me?
- Can I remember the last time I expressed love to myself because I was suffering? How did that feel? And if I can't, can I think now of a situation where I was longing for care and attention because of something lacking inside? Can I now treat myself like my best friend with respect to those circumstances?
- From now on, what is important for me to pay attention to in life? What's not important, and that I shouldn't worry about?
- What makes me unmistakably me?
- What makes me feel alive?
- What do I bring to the world?
- What is my definition of success?

And you can add your own self-inquiry questions below:

_____

_____

_____

_____

_____

Finally, I have selected a resource for you that I find very powerful in connection with this chapter, a short video on purpose, authenticity, and success by Simon Sinek:

https://www.youtube.com/watch?v=eLQ1OXK1V3w

For more, don't hesitate to browse through my "Recommended Resources" at the end of the book.

PART I

Coming from Far, Far Away

*Tell me, what is it you plan to do
with your one wild and precious life?*
—Mary Oliver, *The Summer Day*

*Catania with Etna view from the harbor, Louis-Jean Desprez,
18th century printing (my photo)*

CHAPTER ONE

To Be or not to Be Wonder Woman

Human, Rag'n'Bone

The morning of April 7, 2020 dawned on me like a revelation.

COVID-19 was hitting humankind hard—pretty much everywhere in the world. Brussels was no exception. The word "lockdown" had made its triumphant comeback from grim, distant World War memories... and, worst of all, I could not get up from my bed. I mean, literally.

I swear I tried, and I tried hard. The first unwary attempt to move my left elbow so that I could lift my torso from my lying position, as I used to do every morning, made me gasp with a fiery fit of pain. I fell back on my shoulders with a loud, uncontrollable sigh.

"Here we go again," I whispered to myself, believing I knew what was happening and hence had everything under control. As if two severe back-pain episodes per year on average over 26 years had taught me all about back pain. Today I can relate with tenderness to my wrong assumption, knowing how much I needed to reassure myself. At least, I could easily realize when a blocked spine showed up. Only, this time it felt much worse. Even the slightest move, just a couple of millimeters, would radiate with excruciating pain from my lower back up to my ribcage, shoulders, and neck.

My second thought was, "Damn, I need to tell my team and my boss without delay that I am unable to work."

Of course, a number of more appropriate, measured, wise phrases could have come to mind instead. I don't know, something like "Poor me!", "I feel for you", or simply "Help!" Instead, my Work-Related Sense of Duty, one of the Gods of Guilt, immediately made me feel bad, as if my horrendous pain had not been enough. So much so that I could not think of anything more urgent than calling the office. In my defense, I was leading a team of 20 people, so I was used to feeling the weight of responsibility. Happily Serge, my husband, who as usual was reading beside me in bed, waiting for me to awaken before getting up so as not to disturb my sleep, realized I was going through hell and immediately offered to call the doctor.

You might recall that in those weird days, getting medical help was almost as challenging as climbing Mount Everest. COVID-19 was still a scary, unknown virus, so unless you personally knew a doctor, your call would generally be answered by a recorded message sending everyone to the nearest emergency service for screening. Too bad for someone in my situation! So Serge had the bright idea to reach out for help to a fellow member of his swimming club, Kevin, who also happened to be a physiotherapist. After Serge described the situation, Kevin actually sounded quite concerned. He shared the cell number of his girlfriend, Nicole, and suggested that I call her as a matter of urgency. Nicole happened to be an orthopedist. She was on duty in the emergency department at a well-known city hospital. Its name would strike me later as a fine metaphor for common humanity, where comedy and tragedy often go hand in hand: I had to rush to a Brussels hospital called Molière. When you think that Molière is the most revered French playwright, I bet you will agree with me.

What followed next looked like instructions from "Mission: Impossible" (yes, the movie). Going to the emergency room during the first weeks of the COVID-19 pandemic required stamina, luck, and focus. Like in a videogame, we needed to avoid a series of pitfalls: getting safely to the right entrance (not the one reserved for COVID patients), managing to convince an unwilling security guard to let us into the non-COVID triage line, as I did not want to show that my back pain was hardly bearable, roaming for 10 minutes through completely deserted yellowish corridors before finally finding the right waiting room. Not to mention the torture devices that Serge had just bought, the masks: this situation occurred during the early pandemic phase, when both the press and social media were raging about the usefulness or not of any type of mask in preventing the virus from spreading, and very few people were used to breathing for hours through them. Certainly not us.

Finally I was called in and met Nicole, who turned out to be a pleasant and kind young doctor. She asked me many questions about my pain ("Never experienced anything like this before, even though I have been suffering from regular back pain crises since I was 27"), where exactly I was feeling it ("Between L4 and L5, I know I have a lot of arthrosis for my age, maybe that is the cause, doctor?"), whether I had taken any painkiller ("Yes, Ibuprofen 400, but it did not bring any relief."). Then she sent me to the scanner without hesitation. She would later inadvertently disclose that her first suspicion leaned toward a tumor pressing on my spine. No other cause seemed more plausible to explain the level of pain I was experiencing. Truth be told, even my third child's delivery, which had been the quickest—only 25 minutes—but also the most painful, could not compete with that ordeal.

The advantage of being the only patient at the emergency room (outside the COVID-19 area) that day, during this first lockdown, resulted in my receiving possibly one of the quickest spine scans in the history of medicine, and an equally swift interpretation of results. Doctor Nicole discussed them with another medical specialist to be absolutely certain about the diagnosis, and both formally assured me that it was nothing serious nor dangerous, thus excluding all sorts of tumors, cancers, and the like in the entire scanned region. Having been reassured about a possibility I had not even envisaged, I was really surprised when both doctors agreed that I needed morphine. I had never used any such drug, which in Europe is generally prescribed to cope with extremely severe pain, often for patients in the terminal phase of serious illnesses. I started to realize that the level of pain I was experiencing required more than normal painkillers, under strict medical control. They explained very clearly, for example, that I had to follow the prescribed doses and apply a gradual decrease afterward to minimize the drug's heavy secondary effects. It also felt weird that, in order to take care of myself, I had to use drugs that in different contexts were totally illegal and fed a horrific human exploitation system. I must admit that in a hidden corner of my mind I even felt for a second a sense of mischievous pride for being able to ingest a solid opioid without breaking the law. All in all, I was being required by the medical authority to get the equivalent of the forbidden drug experience I had never been interested in. At almost 53, it felt like I still had a lot to learn.

Incidentally, the two doctors also observed that the scan revealed a very ancient fracture of the hip, likely to have happened very early on in my life.

Later, sitting next to Serge, who was driving us back home, together with a sense of delayed gratitude for not having cancer, the echo of that remark emerged in my mind: a broken hip? For somebody who was already plagued with other imperfections, such as a severe myopia, that was no enthralling news. Could I really have forgotten such an accident, even if I had been just a toddler?

A crowd of disparate thoughts, ranging from "that's why I could never manage a split!" to "I remember my osteopath mumbling something about my asymmetrical hips", assailed my mind.

Soon after, while enjoying the privilege of legal drugs, I managed to gather the energy to call my mom and warily ask her whether she remembered any accident in my young years that could explain my kintsugi[1]-style hip.

"No, I cannot remember any. We never had a car accident, you never fell from a tree, ..."

---

[1] Kintsugi is the Japanese art of mending broken pottery with a golden mixture.

While she was enumerating all possible catastrophes aloud, something she had often told me flashed in my mind.

"Mom, you had a difficult delivery in my case, right?"

"Ha, you can say that! They should have made a caesarian because you were not presenting the head but the bottom. Unfortunately, the doctor was so incompetent that he insisted on a natural birth. I am still bearing the consequences of that decision in my flesh," she sighed.

"So my hip could have been broken at birth."

My mother paused for a moment. I could almost hear her thoughts ticking in her mind.

"You are right! I cannot say it for sure, but it's likely."

That was the gloomy day I was confronted with the medical evidence—and the unsettling, deeply felt truth—that, in spite of all my striving for perfection, I was born flawed. It looked like my relationship to perfection had always been twisted, no matter my desire for it. I could not avoid noticing that this revelation was cunningly embodied in my crooked hip and from the beginning had stripped me of the possibility to become the Wonder Woman I sometimes believed I was.

Of course, there are two sides to perfectionism: a much needed and positive one, revealing itself in the conscientious and responsible striving for the best when carrying out a task or a job, the other side aiming at perfecting our being with the whip of negative self-judgment. In my case, the unhelpful side of perfectionism was recoiling from the discovery that my body was even less perfect than what I thought. Indeed, what could I possibly do to change the situation? And yet, wasn't my body precious in whatever state it was, considering that without a body we would simply cease to be alive?

During the painful weeks that followed that fateful April 7, 2020, the pain gradually decreased, first thanks to the morphine, then to the fact that the inflammation healed and disappeared. Of course, I also needed to follow physiotherapy sessions on video three times a week (remember the lockdown?) and little by little learn to feel my back and hips again. Indeed, for several weeks I kept on experiencing something like an internal earthquake every time I walked: every step made my flesh and bones tremble from inside, a peculiar—and scary—sensation I had never felt before.

I also started realizing that my body was not the only thing that needed care. I was feeling so sad, angry, and discombobulated at the same time, because of what was happening in the world and around us with COVID-19, that I decided to reach out to Helen.

✳ ✳ ✳

Helen was a thin-framed, sporty Czech colleague who boasted a degree in psychology and surprising past experiences, like being a Buddhist nun for six months. She had walked into my office less than one year earlier, saying something along these lines, "Hi, Pinuccia. I am convinced that once I tell you what I practice and can share with you and your team, you will not want to continue our conversation. I am not trained in mindfulness, but in compassion."

OK, this may sound fairly dramatic, but I promise that there were reasons behind such a bold statement.

As a short background, in my organization, the European Commission, it is common practice for managers to organize regular team-building events for their unit. They can address different topics and aim to improve understanding and collaboration in the team. As a manager, I had been trying for some months to organize a team-building day for my team (numbering around 20 people) that would go further than the Belbin test, the Myers-Briggs Type Indicator, and similar widespread management tools. First of all, we had already explored and learned a lot from them in previous team-building events. Secondly, I was personally yearning for something more, that could deepen the good cooperation already present in my unit by embracing all of our human qualities. I was particularly intrigued by mindfulness, which had emerged everywhere in the corporate world, both private and public, as a sort of new management creed. In my organization, some mindfulness courses had been offered to the top management, and staff members had been informed that they could follow individual courses with an external consultant for a fixed price. That made me curious, well before discovering that curiosity, along with mindfulness, is among the qualities of compassionate leadership.

In a serendipitous coincidence, during the first months of 2019 I had been approached by Victoria, a good friend of mine, to take part in collective three-week meditation challenges, and had enjoyed trying those sessions. I had started to experience that meditation basically trains the mind to stay in the present moment, focusing on one thing at a time. I had learned that being fully present in the moment is the very definition of mindfulness. This helps us to refrain from ruminating on past events and feeling anxious about the future, thereby freeing precious time for us to be fully with what is now. I had therefore come to the conclusion that some mindfulness would certainly help even the best teams become more aware, resilient, and effective. I had the intuition that exploring it could bring professional benefits also from the angle of creativity and innovation. However, I would have needed to follow a mindfulness course to get enough knowledge to build the case for organizing a team building focusing on mindfulness—a catch-22 situation. Hence, when I tried to obtain the funds to pay for a consultant to introduce my entire team to mindfulness, the Human Resources department gave a negative opinion. They considered that mindfulness was a catalyst for personal well-being, not a management and team-building activity. So, there was no way for me to organize a team-building event facilitated by an external mindfulness trainer.

As I felt disappointed by that decision, I continued exploring possible alternatives with colleagues working in other areas of the Human Resources department. Then, in August 2019, one of them, Kate, connected me with Helen, a colleague who was also working in human resources and had a rich training in mindfulness and similar subjects. She hoped that Helen could possibly offer us some courses without the European Commission needing to pay an external trainer. I was so excited that I immediately organized a meeting with her.

When Helen entered my office wearing a beautiful, tapestry-like scarf on a dark outfit, I did not imagine for one split second that she would be the catalyst of my inner transformation. No way could I have anticipated that she would instinctively take advantage of the new perspectives on purpose opened in my soul by Sacha, another wonderful colleague, during a special seminar I had followed a couple of months before, and imbue these perspectives with compassion. I will tell you later about that seminar.

As I said earlier, Helen's opening statement included the word "compassion". In her opinion, that word just might make me run away when she uttered it. On the contrary, compassion has connected us deeply ever since. She continued using words that could have sounded sophisticated if she were not the kind of person that embodies simplicity and humanity.

"Compassion means turning to face the suffering, recognizing it in our body, having the courage to face pain, and acting to decrease it. It starts with mindfulness, but goes much further."

I listened carefully to everything she was telling me about compassion, and how it is related to our common humanity. How everybody suffers as a part of our human condition. And how this concerns every aspect of life, including work.

Then she concluded, "I guess you are not interested in this for your team."

I looked right into her eyes and asked instead, "Tell me more. You have really managed to awaken my curiosity."

She glanced back at me with a surprised, almost worried look, and dove deeper into her explanations.

"The Compassion Cultivation Training (CCT) I am trained in is not an easy path; it requires a clear intention to do something to alleviate suffering. People have to be aware of this and consciously choose it."

Helen explained that the course had been designed at Stanford University by the Dalai Lama's personal assistant, Thupten Jinpa, with contributions from the faculty. Both references, to the Dalai Lama and to Stanford, strongly resonated in my mind, at least as much as the word "compassion", which I felt naturally inclined to. The former, because I had enjoyed a brief personal encounter with the Dalai Lama in 2006 in Brussels, during a meeting of EU political decision-makers with spiritual leaders. We had just shaken hands and exchanged a couple of sentences, large smiles, and even a little giggling. I had marveled at his capacity to immediately connect with a stranger like me at a level that allowed us to share some humor. The reference to Stanford also summoned up lively memories: how many times had I dreamed of being enrolled in one of the best universities in the world! When I was 18 or 19, without having the slightest idea of the entry levels required, my hunger to learn and naive self-esteem had brought me to think that only lack of money was standing between me and a world-leading university. This had left a lasting, but unvoiced, regret in my heart. Being taught even only a short course that had been developed at Stanford made CCT feel very attractive to me.

Finally, everything that Helen added to explain the content and the pillars of CCT made it gleam to me. She talked about the importance of settling and focusing the mind, to stop jumping from one thing to the other, and cultivate stillness and clarity of thought. That certainly appealed a lot to me, as I was starting to realize that multitasking had its drawbacks. She mentioned loving-kindness, the quality that enables us to extend benevolence to others. This was a concept borrowed from Buddhism and totally new to me. She added that cultivating loving-kindness would lead us to realize that we all share the same humanity and would open us to compassion and self-compassion, and we would finally start cultivating compassion in our daily life. In the course she envisaged for us, she said she would share her studies, explain some theories, ask us to engage in exercises and practices, and lead meditations. I was totally conquered!

Being an optimist by nature, I was ready to bet that my colleagues would agree to follow what sounded to me like an extremely interesting program. Helen seemed less sure, based on her experience. I told her that I would ask their personal views and do whatever the majority would decide. Actually, to allow everybody in the unit to speak their mind, I asked my secretary to organize a poll, so that colleagues could feel truly free to decline the proposal.

To Helen's surprise, the majority of the unit members replied quite enthusiastically, probably because they were used to my lateral thinking and out-of-the-box suggestions. What touched me was that even the most scientific-minded people accepted, out of curiosity for this strange evolution of the anticipated mindfulness training.

So, we started the course as a team at the beginning of November 2019. The course lasted for eight weeks. Each week, Helen gave a session of 120 minutes at lunchtime to minimize work disruption. Most of my team members followed it quite assiduously and applied at least some of the tools shared by Helen. I was amazed by the generosity and creativity displayed by our trainer, who never missed an opportunity to bring us chocolate, bananas, memorable quotes, lasting truths, and a heart bigger than the sun. She even prepared real participation certificates for each of us and for the unit as a team, and we celebrated her powerful teachings with purple orchids and eternal gratitude.

Then, for a couple of months, life continued to happen as usual. Until it didn't: we had inadvertently stumbled into the COVID-19 pandemic.

Here we were, suffering and pondering the ravages of COVID-19 on our life, work, family, country, continent, and the whole world. I, personally, was painfully going through the worst back-pain crisis of my life, while trying to adapt to a situation where I could not see my colleagues in person anymore. Our IT teams were doing their best but, whenever you put your camera on, chances were that the entire system would shut down. Moreover, everybody was struggling with different issues. Couples with children would invent shifts to make sure one of the parents would take care of their security, basic needs and homeschooling while the other focused on work. Young expatriates felt terribly lonely, and many often found themselves in the impossible situation of having to mourn a close relative without being able to take part in the funeral. And what funeral, by the way? In most countries, funerals were forbidden, along with every kind of gathering, be it for weddings, religious ceremonies, cultural events, or political activities. Millenary rituals were being wiped out by global ripples from a microscopic virus! Most of the time, older staff members would be frightened—and rightly so—by the virus, and avoid all contacts, which in turn could push them into depression. Teenagers would be pushed by feelings of loneliness and isolation into the darkest corners of adolescence, and their parents would feel completely powerless or even desperate. And these were only the most recurring cases.

I decided to reach out to my colleagues whenever the crazy rhythm of the full teleworking mode would allow me to keep our human connection alive and try to soothe, help, support—and at the same time share with them the misery of those dire times.

It was during this troubled period in 2020 that several colleagues spontaneously told me that the Compassion Cultivation Training was helping them a lot. For some it was the breathing practice, for others it was the exercise about really seeing the people around us. A few had started meditating regularly, others realized they felt more empathic than before toward colleagues in difficulty.

Personally, after my back-pain crisis, I had the immense privilege of benefiting from Helen's wisdom twice a month throughout all the mayhem. I had made the bold ask to be coached by her, and she had agreed, teaching me in an understated, unparalleled way how to be more compassionate with myself and to let go of my Wonder-Womanish pretensions. Her coaching style and approach, so refreshing and new for me, cracked my heart open.

So much so that at some point in 2020 I shared a distant memory with Helen. Paco, a dear Spanish friend met during my Erasmus spell in Madrid (an experience that would deserve a whole memoir for itself), had written on my birthday card, back in 1990: "Pinuccia, stop trying to be perfect: being marvelous is more than enough." I told Helen that I had spent many years struggling to fulfill that beautiful wish. Thanks to what I was learning and practicing with her, I could finally accept that I was not perfect and give up on perfection as a life goal. And I embraced the realization that imperfection is just the reality of our human condition. This made me aware that a big change was unfolding inside me.

So, at the dawn of the worst pandemic in contemporary history, the expression of my bodily weakness speaking, screaming through my back pain led me to the traces of a forgotten accident that had broken my hip, thus sealing imperfection into my body. There was no escaping this revelation. I had to mourn the ambition that I could ever be perfect.

This may sound like a quite depressing lesson in itself, but it also shows its silver lining in the moment we realize that we are not alone in being imperfect. That's the moment we connect with common humanity, our common fabric, which is the best antidote I know of against feelings of isolation and loneliness. I, you, each of us share the reality of being imperfect with every single human on our planet. The day we realize it, we start feeling in good company—have you tried?

I finally felt the meaning of the sentence "nobody is perfect" in my body, and little by little I realized that it could free me from the impossible pursuit of absolute perfection. This enabled me to feel much more connected to everyone else, more understanding in the face of human flaws, and eager to build together a viable alternative to the craved, but impossible, state of perfection. Yes, we are free to relate better to other people when we feel that we are part of the same community of marvelous, yet imperfect beings. I could witness this phenomenon also among the members of my team, who have all become more understanding and patient vis-à-vis each other since we followed the CCT course together, during the pandemic and after, when a blended way of working, partly from home, partly in the office, became the new normal.

And yet, it took me five more years to completely flip over my understanding of perfection. This happened when I realized that I would need a new hip. Looks like truth flows through my hips!

Pain began manifesting in my lower limbs from January 2024 onwards. By the summer, it had become so excruciating that I could not enjoy a night of good sleep anymore. It was much worse than when my menopause started, around 2018: in those days, I used to have hot flashes in the middle of the night that would make me wake up in a pool of sweat. Going back to sleep was very difficult, but there was no physical pain involved. This time it was completely different: I spent months suffering at night, with painful fits in my thighs, hips, and sometimes knees and calves. However I was not doing much to decrease my suffering. My unit was barely surviving the pressure of a huge workload, and taking time off to rest would have put them in an even more difficult situation. I did not want to let my team down, and I was hoping, against all odds, that the pain would disappear one day for no reason.

Unfortunately that was not the case. The never-ending pain, coupled with the loss of energy and accumulated tiredness of too many rough nights, brought me to the brink of exhaustion. By the end of November I could hardly put my stockings on, and getting into and out of a car had become an ordeal. I was still taking my beloved dance classes three days a week, even though every time the pain in my legs increased and my nights were becoming more painful. Pushed by my husband and children, who had grown more and more worried about the state of my health, I finally surrendered and sought medical advice. A series of X-rays and ultrasounds revealed considerable osteoarthritis in the pelvic area and a severe inflammation in the left hip. The doctor explained to me that the first step was to treat the inflammation (by medicines first, by cortisone injections afterward if the medicines did not work) and monitor the situation. In case the pain came back, the only lasting solution was a hip replacement. The doctor spoke highly of the operation, saying that it was successful in 95% of cases. Generally, the pain disappeared and mobility came fully back after a few months of revalidation.

Saying that I did not jump with joy at the news is a total understatement. My first reaction was to refuse the idea of the operation. I was angry at the situation and afraid of the surgery. I felt that this bleak development was totally unfair after the toll the pain had taken on me. My internal chatter was judgmental and pitiless: how could my body betray me in such a treacherous way? I had always been reasonable and prudent in my movements and sports choices, I did not deserve this! I could observe resistance, rebellion, and toughness arising in my mind, and I did not realize that the victim in all this was—once again—my poor body.

So, I underwent a first anti-inflammatory treatment that did not succeed in healing the inflammation, then a second, much stronger and longer, that managed to cure it. I felt relieved, and I was back to hoping that this was the end of it.

But hope was not enough to heal me. In February 2025 the pain came back, as intense as ever. I tried a third treatment, but to no avail. I started talking about my issue with relatives, friends, and acquaintances. To my great astonishment I discovered that around 30% of the people I spoke to had already gone through the replacement of one or both hips, or mentioned a dear one who had. That helped me accept that getting a hip replacement was not such a terrible idea, after all. Again, being able to connect to our common humanity enabled me to befriend the possibility that a part of my body be discarded and replaced with a piece of metal.

So, when my mobility and quality of life started decreasing quicker and quicker I surrendered and agreed to undergo hip surgery. It was not an easy process. It required resting much more and for longer than I had imagined. I had to practice patience all along the six months needed for a full recovery. And instead of Wonder Woman, I was nicknamed "Bionic Mamma" by my youngest daughter. A development I had not anticipated!

Since then, something crucial has dawned on me: first of all, that being mad at our body is never a solution. It actually sheds a light on our lack of humility. The moment we ask "why me?" we are actually implying that we don't deserve what is happening, without realizing that nobody else deserves it either. We are all equal in the face of unexpected life developments. It is never a question of "deserving" an issue—be it health, work, family, or about relationships. If we manage to take a step back, we can realize that:

1. The troubling issue can bring us surprising insights.
2. We can learn something new about ourselves thanks to this issue.
3. It is possible to find a new balance in life, one that can increase our awareness of who we are and open up new possibilities for us.

Of course, the three steps do not come automatically and may require much time, suffering, and struggle. However, they bear testimony to our ability to adapt to an infinite range of difficult circumstances and become better through them. In this perspective, can you find a situation in your life that might have some potential to lead you through those three steps? Or a situation that has already done this?

If you are envisaging a hip replacement or have already undergone one, please accept all my admiration and compassion. Common humanity connects us even though we have never met!

To summarize and help you practice, through meditation, journaling, or self-reflection, I have listed here the self-inquiry questions underpinning chapter 1:

- Can I bring to mind a situation where I tried to be perfect? What were the consequences of my struggle?

- Have I already felt how imperfect and wonderful I am? If not, would I feel like giving it a try by visualizing a relevant experience?

- Can I feel that my body is precious in whatever state it is, remembering that without a body I could not be alive?

- If I think of a situation that made me suffer, can I consider that I am not alone in this? What sensations and feelings does this awareness bring to me?

- Can I find a situation in my life with the potential to lead me through the three steps below, or one that has already done this?

    o The issue at stake can bring me surprising insights.

    o I can learn something new about myself through this issue.

    o It is possible to find a new balance in my life that can increase my awareness of who I am and open up new possibilities for me.

And you can add your own self-inquiry questions below:

_____

_____

_____

_____

_____

Finally, I have selected a resource for you that I find very powerful in connection with this chapter, a very clear and comprehensive article on perfectionism, its traps, and strategies to address it skillfully, published on the website called "My Best Self 101": https://www.mybestself101.org/tackling-perfectionism

For more, don't hesitate to browse through my "Recommended Resources" at the end of the book.

CHAPTER TWO

When Unconditional Love Gets in the Way

Somebody, Rachel Druckenmiller

First, a quick word on the geography of my life. You already know that I live in Brussels. What I haven't told you yet is that I was born in Catania (Sicily, Italy) in 1967. I lived in Catania until I was 23, with a spell in Milan when I was aged four to nine. And every location has played a crucial role in my life. Ready for the journey?

So, I was living in Catania when I entered lower secondary school at age 11. From that moment onward I started developing wild fantasies about what I could become as a grown-up. Unfortunately, at no point did I experience an epiphany on this matter. However, I am pleased to report that my imagination displayed a certain degree of originality, as I never dreamt of becoming a top-model or a TV presenter. Those were the most popular dream jobs among my fellow female schoolmates at the end of the '70s. Had my lateral thinking been unconsciously inspired by Sister Andreina's prediction, widely and proudly repeated by both my father and my mother for years?

Let me explain: when I was four my family moved from Sicily to Casalmaiocco, a tiny hamlet in the area of Milan, where we lived for six years before returning to Catania. When we arrived there, my parents enrolled me in the local Catholic pre-primary school. Two nuns, Lucia and Andreina, were in charge of the classroom. I loved going to school and carrying out all the usual educational activities designed for small children together with my fellow schoolmates. In addition, the canteen was so delicious that it left a heavenly smell and taste of *pastasciutta* (pasta with veal sauce) stuck in my nostrils and brain, which later gave rise to a forty-year-long lost-flavor quest, equaled only by a similar quest I conducted to retrieve the unique chocolate taste of the ice cream sold in Catania in the '70s from ancestors of today's food-trucks.

However, one thing I absolutely hated: having to sleep for one hour just after lunch with my head lying on my folded arms, over the table. This detail explains why, even though Sister Lucia was younger and prettier, my preferred teacher was Sister Andreina. Lucia would require me to remain in that very uncomfortable position for the entire hour even though she knew perfectly well that I was unable to rest, let alone sleep (who knows whether my chronic back pain was rooted in that daily obligation!). Andreina, on the other hand, used to wait until everybody else fell asleep, and then set me free to draw, paint, and browse through books. She definitely was a natural-born educator in an era when the academic study of education was less developed than today, as she could instinctively adapt her teaching style to the needs of her very young pupils. I am sure that Sir Ken Robinson, the late British education reformer and most popular TED speaker ever, would have loved her!

This is all that I remember first-hand about my favorite nun. But it is definitely not the only thing that she gave to me. For many, many years afterward, my parents fondly repeated a sentence she uttered at the end of my first pre-primary school year: "This little girl will make you proud", sometimes transformed by the family's oral tradition into "This little girl will go far"—probably because the two ideas were strongly connected in my parents' minds. I am ready to bet she had no idea that this trivial, benevolent expression of her consideration for me would firmly put me on the track of success, as success is commonly understood: top-of-the-class in school and university, landing an impactful and lucrative job immediately after earning a university degree, and making a career with increasing responsibilities, promotions, and recognition. What else?

Now, I never heard her explanation of the above-mentioned prophecy. I am inclined to believe that in a nun's mind such a statement must have involved a measure of spiritual growth. That's probably why it still resonates with me. Anyway, everybody who has watched the HBO *Game of Thrones* series knows that a prophecy may be understood in many different ways, including some that are completely contradictory, until history reveals its true meaning.

So, what was my dream job? This question has no simple answer. From age 11 onwards I doted on a different profession or career every year, going from interpreter to archaeologist, from astronomer to psychologist, with a couple of die-hards: writer and Europe-builder. The latter two would stubbornly stick around, even in the midst of my explosive passion for archaeology, that filled my parents' library with a large number of books on the mysteries of Stonehenge, Cuzco, Machu Picchu, the Easter Island statues, and the like. Writing novels and the European project would creep up during my romance with black holes, quasars, and the theory of general relativity, and both were still nudging me when I decided that my true calling was about the human psyche. That was the moment even my dreams bumped into the wall of reality—and came back with a broken head.

I still remember my excitement while I was mentally preparing for a "serious discussion" with my parents about study choices. I was 18, navigating through a very successful but also frustrating last year in secondary school. It's true that in Italy, just like in Spain, Luxembourg, and Switzerland, to mention just a few examples, you have to undergo 13 years' schooling to access university, while in most Western countries you arrive at the promised land of academia after just 12 years in school. Was this the reason why I was finally bending under the weight of keeping up my first-in-class persona? I can't tell for sure, but it looks likely to me. I was fed up with being always ready to answer any question in class, as this required a level of preparation that was eating up most of my free time. Projecting myself into university thus became a lifeline for me. Finally, I would be allowed to choose the subjects I truly loved to study!

The latest passion I had developed then was for psychology. I felt attracted to exploring and understanding the human mind and our behaviors—and I still am. But finding information on university courses was a herculean task for somebody who was going to be the first in the family to enroll in a higher education institution. No first-hand testimonials, no eyewitnesses, no transgenerational knowledge were available to me. Only the meagre amount of written, summary information I could manage to grasp after long and painstaking research in libraries, browsing paper magazines specializing in higher education studies. So I had sent a request to "La Sapienza" [2] in Rome, the largest Italian university, to get the program of their degree in psychology by mail.

The day I finally received a copy of the study program in psychology I was ecstatic. With long, sensual shivers I read, re-read, and re-re-read the dry sentences about the theories of foreign psychologists such as Jean Piaget, and other amazing subjects, like clinical psychology or statistics. I could picture myself receiving my first clients and helping them ease their pain and solve their lifelong issues. I indulged in imagining myself going to class, totally enjoying the enthralling teachings of inspiring professors, and of course managing to master all the subject matter, as I had always excelled in school. I even wondered why I had not thought about psychology earlier.

My glowing visions, however, could not get rid of a "small" detail that required a serious conversation with my parents: in those days in Italy, only Rome and Padua, which was less easy to reach from Catania, offered university degrees in psychology. Possibly due to the traditional view of psychology then held by most of the Italian population as a waste of time and money, or at best a crutch for mad people, psychology landed very

---

[2] The Italian word "sapienza" translates into "wisdom".

late on the academic menu in my country of origin. My studies would therefore require a considerable financial investment. I was pretty sure my family could afford this, also because my sister had never shown interest in studying and my brother was still a child, so I took the deal almost for granted.

Alas, the discussion went awry in a way I had not imagined. Grounding their observations in fair treatment, my parents told me very calmly and very clearly that my expectation that they would cover the cost of my living four years in the Italian capital was unrealistic.

"We have to be able to support your sister and brother as well, in case they ask for the same. We cannot just give everything to you, hoping that they will not need it. You are the eldest and should understand this. You can go only if you are willing to work and fund your studies by yourself."

All the attempts I made to claim that actually this would be unfair to me, because my sister couldn't care less about university, be it in Catania or anywhere else, and my brother did not come into the picture because he was only six, were rejected without possibility of appeal. I was brimming with rage, because in my mind this attitude was due really to their wish to keep me at home forever. To clarify this point, I have always been the kind of person who, to feel happy, needs to be operational, take action, and have an impact on the world; like a hyperactive bee, I was unable to stop "doing". My days were packed with classes, foreign language courses, poetry club meetings, and modern dance classes, which made my parents regularly complain that I had mistaken home for a hotel. Daytime held the only moments I was allowed to go out without too much questioning: evening and night activities were subject to detailed screening and were limited to a maximum of once a week. Moreover, I had to respect curfew hours that made me a twin to Cinderella. Indeed, I used the word "curfew" in my life well before the pandemic. That's why I could occasionally refer to home as "jail".

I was obviously feeling resentful, because I believed I had earned my parents' support through my total dedication to school, my outstanding results, and my patient attitude toward the strict regulations imposed on my social life. Why on earth should I go and wash dirty dishes in some dodgy bar in a dangerous neighborhood (indeed, I pictured Rome through Pasolini-like eyes) to earn very little money, live miserably, and take longer to finish my degree? Just to please the fairness fantasy of my parents? Moreover, I couldn't have devoted all the time I wanted to studying, which was my real passion, and I could forget about keeping on getting excellent results. This was something important to me, and I could not picture myself lowering my academic standards because of the time I would need to devote to an uninteresting job.

Last but not least, I was convinced that it was just a very low blow on their side, a pure bluff, because they knew me well. It was highly unlikely that I would take them at their word and have a try at the "poor student self-sustaining herself in a big, dangerous, and unknown city" archetype.

Recently, when I explained to my youngest daughter why I could not study psychology at university, she observed that my teenager life was not that easy after all. In her view I had had more than my share of washing dishes and cleaning bathrooms, having contributed to housekeeping since I was eight. It seemed obvious to her that I was not dreaming of this kind of work to make a living and support my studies. That day, I was profoundly touched and grateful to receive the compassion from my own daughter that I had been unable to extend to myself for decades.

The night that followed the argument with my parents, and many nights after that, I simmered with wrath, fuming against what I considered to be their unfair arguments. I finally decided I would do my best to find an alternative solution, enabling me to take full advantage of what they were happy to offer me—in my teenager-like testy words: a golden cage where I was free to study as much as I wanted (minus the time spent on daily chores, of course). Not for one split second did I consider the rebellious option: slamming the door and running into the arms of an unknown, romantic fate. I was much too pragmatic, and I had never been a rebel anyway: why would I start now? My ways were much more those of diplomacy, persuasion, and strategy. And if needed, I could top them off with a bit of a Machiavellian approach too. I was Italian for something, after all!

* * *

So, I needed a plan B. I started recalling the strong impression that my history and geography teacher had made on me, seven years earlier, when explaining how the European project had emerged from the ashes of the Second World War. I had fallen in love with the vision of peace that had brought together nations that had been forever enemies—why would my father still call Germans "those bastards" in the '70s otherwise? Uncompassionate but understandable, I suppose, considering that my paternal grandfather had spent almost two years in Stalag VII-A, according to my calculations most probably between September 1943 and April 1945.

What It Takes to Be Yourself

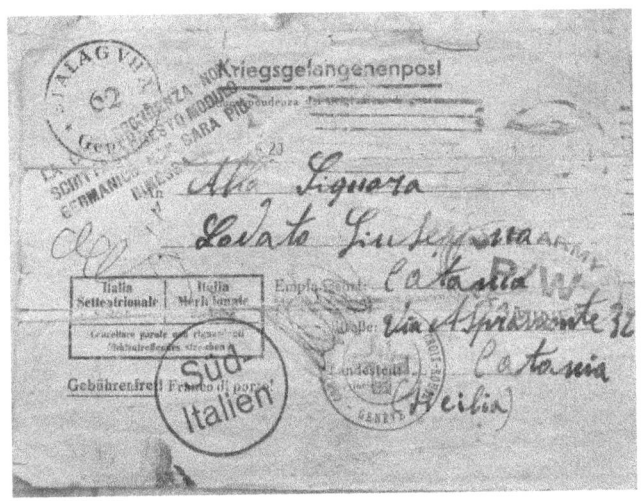

A postcard sent by my grandfather to my grandmother from his prison in Germany (my photo)

Stalag VII-A, in full: *Kriegsgefangenen-Mannschafts-Stammlager VII-A*, situated just north of the town of Moosburg in Southern Bavaria, was the largest prisoner-of-war camp in Nazi Germany during World War II. And of course, not even my father, who was barely seven at the time, could have known this. But happily Wikipedia could. Long live Wikipedia!

We Europeans all bear the wounds of centuries of wars, and the big dreamer I was already at 11 easily imagined herself at the service of that beautiful project as a grown-up.

Following the conflict with my parents about my studying psychology in Rome and my subsequent plan to leave Italy, I became aware that those European dreams were still alive in my heart at 18. It was then that Political Science revealed all its splendor to me. I must confess that was the first time the thought of becoming a student in Political Science entered my consciousness. My memory does not allow me to remember how, but I guess that self-pity and necessity sired that unexpected solution, so that I could focus on an even grander goal than studying in Rome to become a psychologist. I did appreciate feeling in control, even more so when envisioning my future. Life would deal my cards so cunningly that only after decades did I become aware of the limits of such a power. But we will get there in due time.

First, why Political Science among all options? For someone who had previously been attracted to astrophysics and nuclear physics, Latin American archaeology—impossible to study in Sicily, of course—and interpretation—again, feasible only in Trieste at that time, so out of my reach—this might sound like a far cry. It may help to know that I had never been attracted by teaching. Consequently, literature, languages, history, and philosophy—all subject matters I deeply loved—did not look as good choices to me, as they practically earmarked students, and in particular female students, for a teaching career.

Research and academic careers were ruled out too: they were very far away from what I was familiar with. So, I was left with very little. Basically law, economics and political science: separate programs in sociology or anthropology had not yet been set up in Catania at that time. The Political Science degree program of the University of Catania conquered me thanks to its amazing blend of history, economics, law, social science, and foreign languages, which covered almost all my preferred subject areas apart from literature and philosophy. It also offered the possibility of devoting the last two years to international relations, law, and economics, including European-focused subjects. After five years of classics at secondary school, I could sense how such a learning mix would help me complete the pillars of my intellectual understanding of the world. Moreover, the major in European studies I could infuse my degree with would facilitate my professional entry into the European institutions—institutions that had been set up to build and enhance the historic project to rid Europe of war and promote the well-being of its peoples, as beautifully stated in article 3.1 of the Treaty on European Union. That's how I came first to envision, then to decide, that I wanted to leave not only Sicily, but even Italy to pursue a fulfilling career that would enable me to find my breathing space and nurture my personal and professional growth. All this, thanks to a degree in Political Science!

Years later, when I found myself being compared to lawyers and economists at work and felt dismissed as a "generalist", I would remember my mom's youngest sister, one of my beloved aunts, expressing the view that an outstanding student like me was wasted on political science. At that time, both my parents and I felt offended by this actually very relevant remark, even though for different reasons: my parents because they sincerely believed that any kind of studies bore the same intellectual dignity, as I was the first either side of the family to go to university; me, because this indirectly meant that my greatness as a student was not enough to make the studies I chose great.

In hindsight, I have to admit that my aunt's words were full of wisdom in a world that believed in the traditional myth of professional success. As soon as I started working, I was forced to realize how lawyers and economists would immediately be seen as more deserving of authority and advancement than former students of less well-regarded disciplines like me, who were considered children of a lesser God in professional terms. However, I have never regretted my study choice, as I spent four blissful years at the University of Catania, passionately and tirelessly learning subjects that have shaped my vision of the world in a robust, agile, and comprehensive way. And have ultimately provided me with the cognitive tools to continue learning and growing.

Today, I can connect that absence of regret to unconditional love and self-compassion. Indeed, I have never really regretted anything in my life. A bit like the famous French singer Edith Piaf, who sang a beautiful song titled "Non, je ne regrette rien" (literally: no, I don't regret anything). Apart from Edith and myself, I am not aware of many other people who would subscribe to this bold statement, which may mean different things. In my case, it means that I can embrace all my experiences and consider that each of them has brought me value and growth.

I realize this is quite a special trait. And I think I know the reason why: since I was born, I have always felt that God loves me unconditionally. I know, today we are more used to hearing this kind of expressions in Katy Perry's songs than in any normal person's mouth, but I am cheeky enough to reckon that you, my reader, will be intrigued to hear why a modern woman like me, aware of all the horrors of history and of social injustice, would truly believe in such a thing.

Let's first agree that everybody is free to believe in what they want, including not believing at all. Here I am, an Italian woman brought up in a Catholic family in the '60s–'70s, like many others. Several among the young people I knew then lost their faith, others took the step to convert to another religion or embraced atheism. In my case, I was baptized and I am still a practicing Catholic. The fundamental reason for this is that, for as long as I can remember, I have always felt that God loves me as I am. Better, that God designed me the way I am. Nothing less, nothing more. Because if God created me, it must mean that I have some value, otherwise why bother? And I have felt the presence of divine love inside me all along my life journey—which, by the way, also explains why I have never been interested in theories that would reduce sentient and non-sentient beings alike to products of pure chance.

Difficult to believe? Take it from another angle: I could do anything in my life, yet I firmly believe that I could not get to be loved even a tiny bit more or less by God, because in my vision divine love is both unconditional and boundless. So, this awareness becomes my real home—as I bring this shining certainty with me wherever I go—and nobody can take it away from me. I am steeped in God, a God who is infinite love.

Now, this is my personal experience and belief. I realized fairly soon in my life that not everybody shared this view. And that this is normal because we are all different. However there is something that we all share: the wish, a craving for unconditional love, one of the key elements of our common humanity, the fabric we are all made of. The need to be seen, accepted, and valued for who we are, ideally under any circumstance and in every moment of our life. This fundamental need of every human being can be shrouded in religious, philosophical, and cultural beliefs, it can be rooted in a totally secular approach to life or can be simply present in the back of our mind. When we come to fulfilling it, its source can be different for each of us—parents, loved ones, children, nature, the universe, God, you name it.

By the way, what is it like for you? Can you relate to unconditional love in your life experience? Can you name a person, a pet, something that has made you feel loved unconditionally?

In my experience, possessing a clear-cut idea and experience of unconditional love has proven utterly liberating (from any need to fit into a mold), empowering (to be who I truly am), and exhilarating (yes, I can!). However, in my case the strong self-assurance it produced also entailed a good measure of naïveté: in the course of my life, the fact that many people did not share my views about life and love often surprised me, challenged me, and worked to my disadvantage. It took a few rough rides for me to learn how to shield myself from the unwanted consequences of the belief that everybody is good by nature, which I still maintain. And one of the most powerful protective factors in the face of hardship is self-compassion, as Dr. Kristin Neff, a true pioneer in this research area, masterfully explains in her podcasts, academic articles, and books[3].

As you already know, my life shifted toward compassion in the second half of 2019. In January 2021 I decided to enroll in the Applied Compassion Training (ACT) program[4] offered by the Center for Compassion and Altruism Research and Education (CCARE) at Stanford University, following a path that unfolded inside me during 2020 and made me an Ambassador of Compassion (more on this in chapter seven).

---

[3] You will find a host of useful resources made available by Dr Neff on self-compassion at: https://self-compassion.org/.

[4] For more information on the content, structure, and Capstone Projects developed within the framework of ACT, visit the Center for Compassion and Altruism Research and Education (CCARE) at Stanford University website: https://ccare.stanford.edu/applied-compassion-training/.

This extraordinary 11-month-long course was the second of its kind, and it has unfortunately been stopped since 2023. It was offered for the first time as a classroom training in January 2020 and turned 100% online in March of the same year because of the COVID-19 pandemic. This detail was key to my being able to join it in January 2021, as I could not have afforded to travel every month to California to participate in the classes onsite. This program revealed compassion as a core element of my life purpose in the most unexpected way.

The Applied Compassion Training expanded my own perspective on life, happiness, and success because it made me realize and feel in my bones that we all want to be safe, loved, and free from suffering: in a word, happy. It also made very clear to me that the ways we get there are as numerous as the stars in the universe, and each of us walks a unique path that belongs to who we are. Now comes the juicy bit: by definition, this path cannot be a one-size-fits-all. So, if we believe that success is in any way related to our personal happiness, and not only to its social perception, we know deep down that our path to success is unique. And life may lead us there in all sorts of unexpected manners.

During my Applied Compassion Training at Stanford in 2021 I also learned that self-compassion is a quality that Westerners rarely practice for cultural reasons. We are generally much more used to being compassionate and caring for others. But self-compassion is a sort of "mind muscle" that we can develop and cultivate by regularly noticing our own suffering and acting as our best friend would act. These practices significantly help us decrease our suffering. They also make the expression of our self-love progressively more acceptable and easier to feel in our heart.

That's how I have come to realize that self-compassion is the source of unconditional love available to everyone.

✶ ✶ ✶

A surprising opportunity to cultivate compassion toward myself developed over the years thanks to my first name, Pinuccia. Some of you may be thinking right now, "Yeah, speaking of which: first time I've heard it," followed by your personal opinion: how cute, bizarre, sweet, strange, etc. Others might have watched the TV series or read the novel written by Elena Ferrante titled *My Brilliant Friend* and may recall that one of the most important secondary characters in that saga is called Pinuccia.

Personally, for more than 30 years I deeply disliked my first name. Not Pinuccia, which is a short name that I have actually always liked, but my "real" name, the one on my passport: Giuseppa. I can almost see some of you wondering how it is possible to be Giuseppa and Pinuccia at the same time. Yes, indeed, in short: Giuseppa – Giuseppina – Pina – Pinuccia. Four steps to get from Giuseppa to Pinuccia. Italian beats Wordle! Giuseppa was my maternal grandma's name (as you may have noticed in the card sent from my grandpa to her from Stalag VII-A, earlier in this chapter). I had a tender affection for my grandmother. But not even love could counterbalance the fact that already in the good old times, including when I was born, to an Italian speaker's ear Giuseppa would sound heavy and old-fashioned. That's why when I was a child I knew several little girls in Catania who were called Giusy, Pina, Pinella, Pinuccia, Giuni, Jo. Which are all short versions of Giuseppa. As a matter of fact, my best friend in class from age 10 to 19 was called Giusy. Obvious: our grandmothers were both named Giuseppa, so we had received both the name and its... antidote, a cute short name.

I often argued with my father about the name he had decided to give me. My father was unsettled by my constant protests on this point, as he had taken that decision coming from a place of tradition in the noblest sense, as a way to honor our ancestors. On my side, in that decision, which defined me in the most permanent and official way without giving me any chance to oppose it, I was essentially seeing an ugly name that did not correspond to my beautiful being as designed by God. I felt I deserved a more gracious name, and I had built up a list of musical, meaningful, and charming names, such as Myriam, Deborah, or Daphne, that I would have immediately bartered for Giuseppa with no regrets and deep relief.

From time to time, my father would try to stop my recurring whining by saying that he could not do anything about it. Indeed, at that time the Italian law did not permit first-name changes. Strangely, he rarely got mad at me during these recurring arguments, while anger was (and still is) his thing. I suspect it was because the sorrow from my inability to share his deep motives made him feel sad more than angry.

Then, in 2000, the law changed, and I rushed to inform him.

"Finally, I can choose a name that will suit me!"

He very sadly replied, "Be my guest."

As you must have realized, I actually never applied for the legal change of my first name. In the meantime, I had left for Brussels. I had met Serge, the man of my life, who loved the name Pinuccia. And I had connected with so many foreign people who found my name original, beautiful, sweet, and unique, that in the end I simply decided to confine "Giuseppa" to the realm of passports and official documents, and let the world call me Pinuccia.

For some time I reveled in the illusion that my name-curse had disappeared. Until something painful revealed to me that the curse had been lying in plain sight all along. That realization taught me a lesson for life.

During those blissful early years in Brussels, my first name had become music to my ears and a jewel in the eyes of foreigners. However, I had noticed that some Italians would look down on me as soon as they heard my first name. I started wondering why and came to realize that a name like mine could function—together with more explicit cues, such as the university I studied in or my limited travel experience—as an indicator of modest socio-economic origins.

I had been totally unaware that my first name could work as a social identification shortcut for people with my cultural background. This would at times translate into: she cannot play in our category, or even: an outcast not to be admitted into our exclusive network. As Monica Worline and Jane Dutton put it, "It is (...) easy to lose sight of our shared humanity when social barriers begin to divide us."[5]

The hurtful bite of disdain from some of my own folks taught me plenty about how prejudice and social injustice can show up in a covert way. Interestingly enough, it also led me to finally accept that my first name is Giuseppa on my passport and Pinuccia in my daily life. A gift dropped by self-compassion into my heart. Why? Because, as I would

---

[5] Monica Worline and Jane Dutton, *Awakening Compassion at Work: The Quiet Power That Elevates People and Organizations* (Oakland: Berrett-Koehler, 2017), 64.

later learn during the Applied Compassion Training, I went through the following steps:
- I first realized the suffering brought on to me by the snobbish reactions of some Italian acquaintances or colleagues when I introduced myself as Pinuccia;
- I turned to it instead of shoving it under the carpet or minimizing it;
- I felt sorry for myself as if I had seen the little girl called Pinuccia being mistreated for no reason, and I wished good to her;
- The warmth coming from my heart soothed my pain and helped me take distance from the whole situation, including from my own dislike of Giuseppa as a name.

Without my Applied Compassion Training, I could not have described so clearly how I became more self-compassionate and grew with the experience. I could not even have put words on it. Self-compassion is something we are all capable of, as I learned at Stanford and have experienced very regularly ever since; but being aware of it enables us to cultivate it, so that it can become much more impactful. This is one of the seeds that has been secretly growing in my heart since I was a little child, and has become a boundless resource that supports me and gives me strength even in very difficult situations. What about you? If you think of your life, can you recall a specific situation where you offered self-compassion to your suffering self?

Unconditional love has opened its arms to me since I was a little child, and enabled me to dream big. However, it also exposed me to disappointment and hurt until I became more aware of behavioral patterns and social perceptions, learned to feel my suffering, and met it with self-compassion. This awareness and the direct experience of caring for myself have enabled me to attune my original sort of optimism to a more balanced and understanding approach to the world in all its complexity. However, I know of people who have never experienced unconditional love, or have not recognized it when it was offered to them. Does this mean that it only blesses the happy few? Luckily not! Practicing self-compassion has made me aware that experiencing unconditional love is always possible, because self-compassion stems from the deep love we can all express to ourselves.

It is therefore all the more important to become aware of the well of self-compassion that each of us can tap into, because through it we can become aware, recognize, and experience the kindness and, ultimately, the unconditional love every person can express to themselves. I have seen it happening around me, including at work: whenever my colleagues have managed to get to grips with self-compassion, they have realized that this opens up a part of them that generally they had been raised to ignore, mistaking self-compassion for selfishness. This, in turn, decreases their fear of making mistakes and creates new space for creativity and self-expression, thus enhancing not only their well-being but also their job performance. I will tell you more about this later.

Practically everyone can at least offer care and kindness to the self as a child. Would you mind trying, if you have never done it before? You can even look at your preferred picture of you as a child, opening up your heart and noticing the feelings that arise when you contemplate that photo. I am hopeful that you may feel now what unconditional love means, recognize it, or at least approach it from the heart, even if you don't remember having experienced it before. Are there any other people who come to mind who have loved you unconditionally? If yes, you can dwell on that to observe and recognize how it feels to be loved in that special way. And savor it, bask in it, rest in it. It is precious. And it is always available, because nobody can take it away from you.

To summarize and help you practice, through meditation, journaling, or self-reflection, I have listed here the self-inquiry questions underpinning chapter 2:

- Can I relate to unconditional love in my life experience? Can I name a person, a pet, anyone that has made me feel unconditionally loved?

- Do I like my first name (or something else that I consider as a part of me) or not? Why so? What does this reveal to me?

- If I think of my life, can I recall a specific situation where I offered self-compassion to my suffering self? How did that make me feel?

- If I have never experienced self-compassion before, can I think of a situation where I experienced some suffering and offered myself some soothing phrases or gestures? How does this feel in my body?

- Are there any people who come to mind who have loved me unconditionally? Or people whom I love unconditionally? Can I offer the same to myself in a difficult situation? Can I practice it from time to time?

And you can add your own self-inquiry questions below:

_____
_____
_____
_____

Finally, I have selected a resource for you that I find very powerful in connection with this chapter, a video titled "Give unconditional love - Warren Buffett":

https://www.youtube.com/watch?v=bLUPiQHoBgA

For more, don't hesitate to browse through my "Recommended Resources" at the end of the book.

CHAPTER THREE

From Sicily to Belgium with Purpose

Born This Way, Lady Gaga

I have mentioned Serge, my husband, several times in a previous chapter, but he deserves more, much more than a hint here and there. Not only because he is the man of my life, my perfect match, the Prince Charming whom I had been waiting for my whole life—I mean, until I was almost 24. Indeed, I was lucky to stumble upon him so early. Or, better, I was filled with so much faith in and dreams about the man who had been created and destined for me (and vice versa), that I am ready to bet God thought I would go mad with longing and craving, had I been obliged to wait any longer. However, this is a topic for another memoir altogether.

My problem here is that there is no way to describe Serge in full. Not merely because he is—literally—the best, kindest, most intelligent and impressive man I have ever met. Okay, I have not met millions of men, but a good number for sure, and from very different backgrounds. But taking into account the widespread Italian propensity to worship beauty and intellectual gifts, those to whom I felt attracted were generally handsome and fit, spoke at least four languages and sported outstanding intelligence and academic degrees. Not that I consciously intended to exclude the bad and the ugly (the spaghetti western movie featuring Clint Eastwood might be ringing a bell here). My heart simply jumped at any boy or young man boasting a novel combination of these four qualities, which totally deprived me of common sense and left me to discover, in due time, whether that particular guy truly deserved my passionate love. Other parameters to be factored in, and which required deeper investigation, were: a good heart, courage, and an artistic calling.

Yes, art: I discovered relatively quickly that the initial four magic qualities would promptly bore me to death without a measure of art—and humor. But not any sort of humor, please: unlike Stephen Fry, whose type of humor I cherish, Mr. Bean would never conquer me, even though I must admit that the latter's ways are very creative.

The final, decisive element was the reply to the question: will he clean the toilet?

To clarify this last element of the equation, I need to rewind back to when I was 14. It was a normal day at home in Catania, and I was helping my mother make her bed. As we had always both been of the chatty type, we were talking about my ideal man.

"You see, mom, I could never marry somebody like dad."

"Don't be silly!" she replied, visibly shocked. "Your dad is the best man on Earth."

"As a dad, mommy. Not as a husband."

"What do you mean? He is a good man, hard worker and responsible. He is honest and gentle. He is a man of faith, fair, and generous..."

I had to interrupt her.

"Indeed. But he would never clean the toilet."

She laughed at me.

"Why would he need to clean the toilet? I can do that!"

"That's not the point, mom. I want a man who has no problem in doing the same things I do, and is happy with me doing whatever I want."

"You don't want a man, you want a little dog then!"

"Seriously, mom? Why would women be allowed to only do certain things? Why should they always do what society and tradition have imposed on them for centuries?"

"Because of the different nature of men and women! You don't have the power to change that. And in any case, you will never find an Italian man ready to clean the toilet."

"You are right, on this we totally agree. That's why my husband will most probably be a foreigner."

My mother had not seen that coming. Her face lost its color, and she remained speechless for a few seconds. Then she rebounded and fired back.

"In such a case, don't count on my appreciating him. What kind of man would agree to clean the toilet?"

I felt excited and very sad at the same time. Excited, because I had clearly won the argument: I have always loved winning a fiery battle of opinions! Sad, because my own mother could not understand my craving for a truly equal relationship. I knew I had plenty of gifts and talents: apart from the famous Sister Andreina's prophecy that I would go far in life, I had always loved learning, devoured novels, and developed a passion for languages. Being recognized as the best pupil at every school I had attended, be it in Northern or Southern Italy, had taught me a couple of things about the fact that nothing can justify discrimination, and had reinforced my innate self-esteem and self-love. Then, why should I find myself confined within the same life paradigm as my mother, my aunts, and their female friends: all busy with housekeeping and children's upbringing? Very few of them had ever had a job, and it was generally because they needed the money, not because they loved what they had to do. Moreover, those who worked were plagued with endless remorse and a sense of guilt, as having a regular job necessarily meant being a lesser mom, spouse or daughter than those who were "lucky enough" to devote their life entirely to the family.

This picture was very far from what I wanted. Of course, I also dreamt of my Prince Charming and having kids, of surrounding myself with the beauty of a lovely home, the warmth of a blissful family and all that went with it. However, my vision for the future started with making the world a better place directly, through a meaningful and well-paid job, aligned with my intelligence, values, and talents, and not just indirectly through a happy family. I was bold and confident enough to believe I could achieve the part of this vision that depended on my efforts, while I felt much less sure that the man of my dreams would automatically materialize out of them. I could already see the difference between what I could reasonably count upon attaining based solely on my own forces and what instead required a rare alignment of planets to happen.

For sure, I had clear ideas already in my young years about what I wanted and why. However, when it comes to my life purpose, I cannot say that I had given much thought to it at that time. Purpose would strike many years later, and tease me for some time before revealing all its cards. This would change my life from the inside out.

What was keeping my mind busy and my heart pumping in my dire teen years (hands up, any of you who can honestly say you were a happy teenager) was the irresistible dream—and conviction, because I happened to feel absolutely certain about it—that I could have it all: a unique, long-lasting, and happy love story with the man that God had designed for me (and me for him) from a time before the Big Bang, including the toilet cleaning feature; a harmonious family, with as many children as we pleased, each of them being a unique masterpiece; a meaningful and interesting job where I would totally enjoy every minute, do something great to improve the world, and be paid well enough to be able to afford everything I fancied (excluding trips to the Moon, planes, and yachts, let's immediately clarify); and, as a final touch, beauty, elegance, and warmth everywhere in and around me.

The good news is that today I can subscribe to and tick every single word of the paragraph above, representing my own definition of success.

The bad news is that it took me 30 years to realize that happiness, what I was really craving, was actually hidden, and sometimes buried, under this glowing pyramid. Because for success and happiness to coincide, I first needed to unravel whatever myth about success I had absorbed in my young age, pull its elements apart—academic degrees, social status, money, recognition, fame, family, travels, you name it—and seriously consider what was left. Then, and only then, did I start discovering all the gems that lit up my path, until I could connect the dots, weave the lines together, and feel happiness right down into my bones. Finally realizing that what mattered most to me—success on my own terms—was to increase my overall happiness and wisdom. And understanding that this happens when we are authentic, meaning truthful to our true essence, to the unique, imperfect, and marvelous gift each of us represents for humankind—which, by the way, is also in my view the best path for us to be genuinely appreciated by other people.

Purpose is one of the pillars of authenticity. Indeed, how can we be who we really are if we are not aware of what we can bring to the world? The beauty is that everybody has purpose in life; the challenge lies in becoming aware of it. Purpose was already there when I stubbornly devoted the hundreds of hours I spent in traffic, driving back and forth from my family's apartment on the outskirts of Catania to the university buildings in the heart of the city, to improving my language skills by talking aloud to myself in English, French, and Spanish. I bet you have never heard of a weirder way to become fluent in three foreign languages! Purpose nourished my decision to study Latin and Greek in secondary school—a choice I share with the former UK Prime Minister Boris Johnson, but for different reasons: he jokingly observed once that he did it because only privileged people study useless subjects, while I deeply loved those dead languages that opened up the doors of philosophy, history, and law to me.

What It Takes to Be Yourself

My upper secondary school nameplate (my photo)

Early in my life, it was purpose that pushed me to painstakingly study even the subjects I did not really like, as I considered that I might need that knowledge one day. OK, to be completely honest, it was probably also my hubris, as in those times I held my IQ in such high esteem that I felt I could be good at studying anything. I have learned all along the way since then that being good at many things does not really help when you need to understand what exactly you have come to do on Earth. Anyway, purpose made me a philosopher at seven and a mystic at eight, dropping bombs of meaning and enlightenment on me whose shards remained dormant in my soul for decades. What, other than purpose, could possibly convince me that my path had to cross the center of Europe when my roots were firmly steeped in Italy?

✳ ✳ ✳

After a long and winding road, purpose eventually officially introduced itself to me. This serendipitous encounter took place in July 2019, when

I embarked on a thrilling adventure called a "walking seminar on life purpose". Let me now—finally!—introduce you to Sacha.

Let's clarify first that Sacha is a man—as you may know, Sacha is one of those intriguing names that can be given both to boys and girls. Just like Dominique, or Kim. And the beauty is that he was called that way because his maternal grandma was a Ukrainian lady named Sacha. The Sacha I will tell you about is one of the very few straight men I know who are both aware and proud of their feminine side.

Sacha is one of those people who are genetically Europeans before being anything else. Not even I could be counted among the members of this club, as my Sicilian lineage had interrupted its international intake at least one century before I was born. But, going back, it actually spans more than Europe, as it includes Phoenicians and Greeks, Romans and Arabs, Normans and Spaniards—before we finally come to the Italians. Sacha's ascendants, besides Ukrainians, include Italians and Belgians, who have granted him his nationality. A really rich mix!

I had met him for the first time at the end of 2018. At that time, I felt a strong desire to do more in my organization to nourish my commitment and counterbalance the feeling that my promotion chances to senior management were dimming (I'll tell you more on this later). This development had led me to volunteer for a new human-resource-stamped initiative: the set-up of the corporate middle managers' network. I had immediately appreciated Sacha's kind and candid look during the first get-together of the network's core group members, and we had exchanged a couple of deep thoughts about what we both agreed to be at the root of the European project: replacing war with peace and prosperity. Forever. That had been enough for me to know in my bones that he was one of the good guys.

When I learned, some months later, that he had voluntarily stepped down from his managerial position to serve as a trainer of managers, I was only half-surprised: to me, he certainly stood out as somebody with a deep European conviction and a profound spiritual life. I could sense how his personal growth path was unfolding in ways that distanced him from the predominant career benchmark at the Commission—and more generally in the corporate world— that equated promotion with success, demotion with failure, and voluntary stepping down with weakness. During a conversation we held in the Parc du Cinquantenaire, close to the Berlaymont building, the Commission's headquarters in Brussels, sitting together on a pine-green bench under a sprawling beech, he shared with me what had motivated him, and how much that made him brim with energy, for which he earned my ever-lasting, sincere admiration. He also made me a standing offer: if ever I would feel the need to give up on my managerial functions to follow my deeper calling, I could join his team. I have not forgotten that offer, for which I will always be grateful to Sacha. It felt like a safety net to me, and it has made my personal journey and choices even more assured ever since.

Then, in July 2019 I enthusiastically volunteered to take part in one of the first walking seminars for managers, a training prototype that he had designed to bring to the surface the life purpose of every participant and provide new inner resources to managers coming to a key stage of their professional career.

We started as a group of ten from different European institutions, including eight managers (four men and four women) and two trainers: Sacha and another sweet colleague from the Human Resources department, Kate. Yes, the one who would, soon after, connect me to Helen. Crazy, right? The three-day walk started on a bridge decorated with sculptures of colorful saxophones in Dinant, the Belgian town where their inventor, Adolphe Sax, was born, and ended under a fig tree in the garden of an ancient abbey that lends its name to one of the most famous Belgian beers, Leffe. During those enthralling days we all tasted and experienced poetry, painting, storytelling, and contemplation. We told each other truths we had not been aware of, were blessed with enlightening moments, and had more time to reflect on the meaning of our life than in the previous ten years. Believe me, there was no way back from the emotional, psychological, and spiritual growth most of us experienced in just 72 hours. By the way, and for the sake of clarity, here is what I mean by spirituality, following the definition shared with the soon-to-be ACT Ambassadors of Compassion by one of my beloved teachers, Neelama Eyres: a sense of connection with something greater than oneself. The something in question can be called God, the divine, the universe, nature, humanity, sports, arts, beauty, you choose. What counts is that spirituality is a universal aspect of the human experience; fMRI (Functional Magnetic Resonance Imaging) has even shown its place in the brain[6]!

---

[6] If you want to read more about the science of spirituality, check out this article: Alison Escalante, "Scientists Think They Just Found The Brain's Spirituality Network," *Forbes*, 24 August 2021,
https://www.forbes.com/sites/alisonescalante/2021/08/24/scientists-think-they-just-found-the-brains-spirituality-network/.

What It Takes to Be Yourself

Spirituality is therefore another element we humans have in common. Another thread in our common fabric.

With all of this happening, by the end of the walking seminar I had promoted Sacha to the rank of prophet. I am sure you are wondering why. Traditionally, prophets say things that are difficult to hear and even harder to implement—have a look at the Bible or *Game of Thrones* if you don't believe me. Very often they lead complicated, if not miserable, lives and, apart from lucky guys such as Elijah, who was elevated to Heaven on a chariot of fire (what a cool way to scare death off!), most of them die violently or in very poor conditions.

Be reassured, these were not the reasons why I pictured Sacha as a prophet. Prophets generally lend their voice to the something greater than ourselves referred to above, and for sure what he had to tell me was much bigger and deeper than smart-sounding statements crafted for an innovative training course for managers. With his gentle, nudging style, leading the group in the most creative and inclusive way, he managed to extract us from the daily craze of multitasking and obsessing over urgencies, and he had us bathe in our life purpose: something greater than us, something that permeates and gives meaning to everything we do. And yet, we might spend our entire life not noticing it, because actually we are living inside it. Like air and gravity.

That experience increased my awareness of purpose and allowed me to get closer to representing and describing my life purpose. I knew I wanted to be together with others, to have impact so as to make the world a better place. By the end of the three days, I had drawn a colorful coat of arms including three different images: the first depicted the sea, the sun, a playful dolphin, a blue sky, and flying birds to express freedom and love of nature. The second pictured a lighthouse on a rock to represent positive impact and leadership. The third showed an EU blue flag with its twelve yellow stars embracing the world as a reference to the European project and its global impact. The words that came to me to summarize my life purpose were "together, impact for the greater good".

The coat of arms representing my life purpose that I drew in July 2019 (my photo)

Before the walking seminar I would have been ready to swear that I knew everything about my life purpose. In those days the limited perception I had of my life purpose rested heavily on my professional career development—as if a promotion, a new title, and a couple of hundred euros more in my pocket had the power to make me become more of myself. So, I considered my partial life purpose motto as an awesome result, well worth even the 40 km we had to walk through the woods on a very hot end-of-July day in the Belgian hilly region called the Ardennes.

What It Takes to Be Yourself

※ ※ ※

The following two years would fill in the blanks and reveal the core of my life purpose that had remained undercover in Leffe. And Sacha would keep on being my prophet friend. However, before lifting the curtain on the complete version of my life purpose, I need to unveil what really brought me to try out something as unlikely as a walking seminar on life purpose. Truth is that by July 2019, I had given up on my attempt to quit the European Commission. Yet, I was craving a new quest in my life.

Sorry for the low blow. I am pretty sure you had not seen that coming. Why would a mother-of-three and pragmatic manager envisage giving up on the status, money, and influence she had earned over 25 years of hard work? The short reply is that I had been feeling undervalued and not "seen" for years. You'll discover why later. For now, let me focus on my attempt to find another job.

The main thing that I learned through the experience of trying to quit the Commission was that nobody outside the circle of EU experts, counterparts, and stakeholders actually knows what we do in our work. Difficult to picture? Let me indulge in a metaphor. Imagine you have been living a passionate, sensational life as a spy—yes, a spy—for 25 years. You know how hard, challenging, unnerving, and devastating it has been to act according to your legend, putting yourself in the shoes of some unassuming average citizen, be it a flower shop owner, a school teacher, or a tailor, paying constant attention to become one with your mask, while living on stand-by around the clock—and occasionally having to leap from the window onto a rubbish bin, use your karate moves against a mysterious killer, or fly an airplane trusting your 20-year-old pilot training memories.

Then, after getting an imitation gold-medal to celebrate your secret career and reluctantly giving up on your promotion dreams for good, you bravely decide that you want to close this chapter of your life and use your transferable skills in a sector, or industry, that must surely be longing for someone with your spectacular and unique talents. You feel energized and optimistic, because, of course, like everybody else, you have watched James Bond's adventures, and you realize you crave a life in the open.

You are good at networking and get a first appointment with a headhunter. You introduce yourself, give her your resume and in three minutes you explain all the wonderful aptitudes and abilities you have cultivated and brought to their fullest expression in decades spent as a secret agent; you have learned to do this in very expensive executive programs organized by Ivy League universities, maybe while faking a life as a hospital director. You end on the high note that obviously your long-honed skills "must be badly needed in all the areas where a comprehensive strategic vision, coupled with a strong drive for action, and proven problem-solving capacities in highly complex environments are a definite asset."

In the meantime the headhunter's look, let's call her Virginia, has gone from enthralled to puzzled and finally annoyed, because she now has to explain to you, in a polite but clear way, that she cannot do much for you. She will probably start congratulating you on your awesome spying career and note that undeniably you have a unique profile. Then she will prudently introduce the argument that extraordinary profiles like yours are very inspiring. At the same time, they develop in contexts which are estranged from usual, more down-to-earth workplaces like the corporate world, banks, insurances, consultancies, companies, and the like. She will continue regretting the lack of imagination of most Boards and top managers, who actually seek first and foremost to be reassured by typical resumes and well-known, recognizable career patterns. As she is likely well-intentioned and does not want to make an enemy of you, she will conclude that she will of course keep your file and contact you in case the unique vacancy matching your unique profile comes up.

You leave the classy, shiny head-hunting office behind you with a feeling of joyful expectation. It's only when a whole month passes by with no sign of life from Virginia that you start grasping the full meaning of what she said.

In case you are still wondering, let me put things straight: I have never worked as a secret agent. Maybe you have? (I'm getting curious here.) Personally, I have been acquainted with American, Russian, British, Israeli, and French spies only on screen. And can you, my dear reader, pretend you know something about real spies, unless you are one of them, in which case you cannot disclose your true identity? My point here is that outside the Commission world hardly anybody knows what we do or how we work. Not because we behave like spies or cannot talk about what we do; but because we can impact plenty of very important things in the economic, social, and legal spheres, quietly—the entire Commission employs less staff than the City Hall of Paris. Additionally, in order to understand our daily activities you need a PhD combining law, history, and international relations. No joke.

Between 2017 and 2019, I indeed went through the same trajectory of soul and job searching as my atoning spy avatar, talking to a number of head-hunters in Belgium, France, and even Canada. I held intense conversations with former corporate top managers turned professional coaches. I travelled abroad to meet with impressive and empathetic CEOs, friends of friends of mine who had asked them to benevolently listen to me and give me their valuable advice. What I discovered in these meetings, often taking place in posh restaurants and trendy bars, was a lot about the meanders in career paths, employment benefits and office politics in the corporate world. I was surprised to realize how similar their patterns were to those I was familiar with in the European Union circles, and at the same time how completely separate those two worlds remained. A bit like trying to change from a non-profit to a corporate job in the US.

Lots of sympathy and interesting anecdotes filled those special encounters. However, no job offers ever materialized, directly or indirectly. Moreover, as I was piling up contacts, connections, phone calls, meetings, and working lunches/dinners, my thinking became clearer and clearer. I had started my search with the firm belief that I could easily find a well-paid job in practically any industry sector, thanks to my 25-year long experience in the multicultural, complex, and challenging world of the European institutions. Aren't all multinational companies similar animals? How naive! My initial equation had three assumptions: it would be easy for me to find a job outside the European institutions; I might maybe even get a better paid one, as I felt undervalued in my organization; and I would be able to choose something that embodies my values.

Slowly but surely, I realized that each of them was false. Firstly, finding a solid job outside my professional world would require an inordinate amount of networking, trials and error, and investment of time and energy on my side. Secondly, whatever job I could find, it would not pay as well as my current one. Not to mention that I had never needed to negotiate my salary. Basically, in the European institutions increases in salary can come only through promotion, and this involves very specific procedures. Every step up on the career ladder comes with the same exact salary increase for everybody. So I had never needed to fight for money, according to the blessed law of laziness. I mean that our brains prioritize what we really need to learn for survival purposes, to spare our limited energy. This is one of the winning attitudes that has saved our species from extinction. Moreover, I could not even dream of setting up my own company: even a lean one-person consultancy would require a couple of years of net investment, and I simply could not afford it.

Finally, the only sectors that would maybe deign looking at my credentials for more than a second were NGOs and charities, as in that period of my life I still believed that what makes a job noble and worthy is not the attitude and intention you put in, but first and foremost its "nature". And, having served the European Union day-to-day for 25 years, I had decided to exclude from the start all public policy roles, which for me at that time was just an elegant name covering all sorts of lobbies "courting" the European authorities.

Later, while studying compassion and practicing it in my everyday life, I realized that judgment and prejudice can block compassion in many unexpected ways. I had been suffering because of others' prejudice against my socio-economic origins and the kind of studies I had chosen. Yet, I too was wrapped in unconscious bias when it came to considering business sectors, as I would assess some as better "by nature" than others. The fact that unconscious bias may happen in all areas of life was not an excuse for me to indulge in it, of course, and little by little I became aware of this and took measures to counterbalance it. However, the question remains: why do we think that some jobs are better than others? Maybe because we are so exposed to conceptions of success that prevail in our circles, communities, or culture that we instinctively compare and rate jobs on a pre-determined scale of value, losing sight of the fact that a job is just a job. What really makes the difference is how much it corresponds to who we are, and whether we fulfill it in a spirit of service or not.

So, I had to reconsider the entire plan. It was unnerving, because it forced me to give up the splendid revenge plan that would have allowed me to quit my employer royally, slamming the door, and snickering in the face of all those who I felt had underestimated me. I therefore fiddled for some time with the idea of applying for a research fellowship at Berkeley (there was a small opening there reserved for experienced European officials), but Serge managed to talk me out of it. Competing for it would have required months of heavy investment on my side, and even if I had been granted it, this would have meant:

- moving the family with me for ten months to California,
- writing a solid academic article and offering master-level classes while desperately trying to find another job,
- accepting the prospect of coming back to the same job I had left in case I did not manage to land somewhere else.

The only things I could be sure of were uncertainty, lots of extra work due to the move, and much, much more work, stress, and anxiety. I realized it would have been nonsensical to get all of us into this, while I had been looking forward to increasing my level of happiness with my next professional move. That brought me back to square one. I felt like a lioness in a cage. I was totally stuck in my apparently privileged, possibly envied position in the European Commission.

But what if the only path I had not tried yet was the good one? What if, instead of striving to upend the world I had been living in, I started to change the way I looked at it from the inside?

Here I have to tell you that there was no "Aha!" moment in which I begot such an uncanny manifestation of wisdom. The only thing I remember is my Coach Number One (this is how Helen always called Serge, considering herself to be my Coach Number Two) telling me at some point, "Pinuccia, stop banging your head against the wall: there's no way out." But even my husband's clear message could not prevail over my stubbornness. However, wisdom trickled to me drop by drop, first, as you may remember, through the unlikely invitation to start a 21-day-long meditation challenge by Victoria, and then via the post on the Commission's intranet that lured me into Sacha's walking seminar on life purpose.

When I think of that summer of 2019, a summer like no other one for me, I feel like a Tarocco orange. No, I am not attempting to compete with Dustin Hoffman trying to play a tomato at the beginning of *Tootsie*. I simply cannot resist this comparison. First, because this type of orange grows only in the part of Sicily where I come from: Catania—and more specifically the slopes of Mount Etna, my dearest volcano. So, no cultural appropriation here: I belong to "Taroccoland" as I was born there, just like my beloved oranges. Second, because the unique characteristics of this very special fruit—its unmistakable sweet-and-sour flavor, its patchy orange skin, its inside, made of small bags of juice in all the nuances of red and orange, like a tequila sunrise—could be a great metaphor for my evolution since then. Actually, Tarocco oranges ripen during the winter, and the different shades of orange and red inside are the response of the fruit to the nocturnal microshocks inflicted upon it by sudden drops in temperature after sunset: Mount Etna is the highest active volcano in Europe, standing 3357 meters (11 013 feet) tall. This specific kind of weather, combined with the volcanic soil, creates a secret harmony that can only be tasted in full once you have looked at the skin, opened it, peeled away the whitish sour substance that protects each slice, and finally put the slice in your mouth. Then you can start chewing it with your eyes closed, breathing in its smell while you experience its exquisite taste.

Why am I bringing Tarocco oranges into the picture now? Because, just like them, purpose and compassion were tiptoeing their way through my life day after day, with microshocks comparable to the chilly winter night temperature drops on Mount Etna. And this was shaping a more authentic, liberated and happy version of me, able to be better and more helpful to the people around me.

What It Takes to Be Yourself

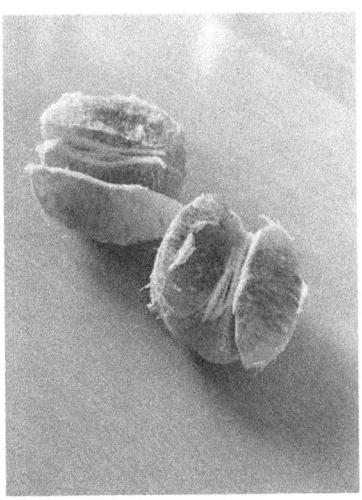

Tarocco oranges on my kitchen table (my photo)

No wonder I can eat one kilo of Tarocco oranges a day—if you only let me.

And what about you? If you were a fruit, which fruit would you be? Can you see how fruit can be a metaphor of who you are? And what feelings does this image bring to you, into your body?

Let me also share with you a tool that I have developed based on what I have studied and experienced about purpose as a foundation of authenticity. Because uncovering your purpose and becoming aligned with it empowers you to be yourself fully, in every moment of your life. I have tested it on hundreds of participants in my purpose-themed sessions, and the feedback I have received has been extremely positive.

I like to call this tool, consisting of five simple, deep questions, a "purpose refiner", because purpose is a process, it can change and evolve, and what counts is that we become more aware of it little by little. Here are the questions:

- What are your passions?
- Are you good at them?
- Are you willing to invest in these passions to become better at them?
- What is the added value you will bring to the world through this?
- Who will benefit from it, or be your audience?

I have often been asked what I mean by "passion": actually, anything (an activity, an interest, a hobby, an art, a habit...) that makes you feel at home, safe, fulfilled, and energized, something you can never have enough of. If you are not that good at these passions, or you are not ready to continue investing to hone them, you are not getting closer to your purpose but you have stumbled upon another precious asset for your well-being: your resources, which can be physical, emotional, cognitive, or spiritual. These activities are the best ways to help you recharge your batteries and nurture your resilience. So this tool, the purpose refiner, has a by-product that you also want to know and cherish, because resources will come to your help whenever you are running low on energy or going through difficult times.

Once you have identified your true passion(s), you can keep on approaching your purpose through the questions below, focusing on added value and your audience/beneficiaries. It may take a long time, you may arrive at a first definition of your life purpose and then change it, or maybe you will keep asking yourself certain questions. Any response coming from your inner wisdom is good and will help you get more clarity. In my case, the tagline I have come to consider as my life purpose, at least for the moment, is the following: manifesting unconditional love and growing compassion together for the greater good.

And maybe thanks to the purpose refiner you will have a smoother journey than Tarocco oranges to authenticity!

To summarize and help you practice, through meditation, journaling, or self-reflection, I have listed here the self-inquiry questions underpinning chapter 3:

- Can I bring to mind a situation or a memory that connects me to my life purpose? How do I feel in my body when I do so?

- In which situation(s) have I felt authentic? Can I recognize the emotions that emerge in my body when I experience authenticity?

- What can I bring to the world?

- What if, instead of striving to upend the world I have been living in, I started to change the way I look at it from the inside? Can I practice it on something small? What does the practice teach me?

- If I were a fruit, which fruit would I be? Can I see how fruit can be a metaphor of who I really am? And what feelings does this image bring to me, into my body?

- Finally, here comes the "purpose refiner":
    - What are my passions?
    - Am I good at them?
    - Am I willing to invest in these passions to become better at them?

- What is the added value I will bring to the world through my passion and continued investment in it?
- Who will benefit from it, or be my audience?

And you can add your own self-inquiry questions below:

_____

_____

_____

_____

Finally, I have selected a resource for you that I find very powerful in connection with this chapter: a morning meditation for greater vitality, purpose, and intention made available by Fleur Chambers on "Insight Timer": https://insighttimer.com/thehappyhabit/guided-meditations/morning-practice-for-greater-vitality-purpose-and-intention

For more, don't hesitate to browse through my "Recommended Resources" at the end of the book.

PART II

Finding Self-Fulfillment at Work

Be yourself—everybody else is already taken.
—Oscar Wilde

A gorgeous sunset after a storm in Brussels (my photo)

CHAPTER FOUR

Humility, the Underrated Power

Titanium, David Guetta (ft. Sia)

I promised I would not transform this book into a teenager-ish romance, so don't take me wrong if I still need to tell you something which belongs to the period when I started dating Serge.

The day I broke the news to my parents that Serge and I were in a serious relationship was the equivalent of Armageddon in their life. Later they would share with me how they spent sleepless nights weeping over my fate and worrying for their eldest daughter. I clearly appeared to them to have gone completely crazy. How could I decide out of the blue that I had met the man of my life and start living with him? Without even asking for advice! With no trusted person in sight who could check, consider, test, analyze, and report back on this stranger! It must have been the devil in person, as the Pinuccia they knew was a devout, balanced, and reserved girl who would never run into such reckless ways.

What followed was my family's version of eating humble pie: I had to immediately book a flight to Catania and promise that I would go alone, to enable my parents to properly examine the state of my mental health. That was not a problem for me, as Serge was already plotting to join me a couple of days later, after I had exhausted their initial objections, in order to ask my father for my hand in marriage as in the good old times. He reckoned that this flattering gesture alone would flabbergast them and buy him their consent. Like mischievous children, we had giggled together picturing the face they would pull the day he would knock on their door, and they would see him standing right in front of them, 2300 kilometers (1400 miles) from Brussels—as a matter of fact, as soon as he arrived, he conquered them altogether. I was, however, less inclined to giggle when I discovered that one of the reality checks my parents had in store for me was a meeting with Father Tommaso.

Father Tommaso was a stark, balding priest who directed the community of the *Padri Passionisti* (literally, Passionist Fathers) serving at a shrine dedicated to Our Lady of Sorrows and located some eight kilometers (five miles) further up on Mount Etna from where my parents live. He was a long-standing spiritual and moral reference for my family. His inquisitive eyes, long nose, and pointy face made me think of a mouse whenever I met him. Notwithstanding this, I had spent some time during my studies writing for the community's newsletter under his direction. I knew perfectly well that a close encounter in the current circumstances would not bring anything good, because of his traditional approach to religion and the role of women in society. However, I felt obliged to accept my parents' request in order to reassure them that I had not lost my mind in Belgium, and I was foolish enough to think that I could touch him with my tale of love at first sight in a distant country.

When the secretary let me in after announcing my name, he was seated at his massive wooden desk wearing the official black, long robe that he generally traded for a simple T-shirt and cotton trousers, much more appropriate when facing the extreme heat of a Sicilian summer. It was the first time he had not stood up at my arrival, thus leaving no doubt that my situation was particularly serious and required special treatment. The severity of his look was compounded by the deep wrinkles in his forehead, looking like ruts in a dry field. What a contrast with the wide smile he generally displayed to welcome me! My heart raced, I felt like I was entering the Inquisition interrogation room.

Father Tommaso did not offer any gesture to put me at ease. On the contrary, he barely said hello and immediately started to address me and my sins in an unforgiving tone.

"What you have done leaves me speechless."

(What was I guilty of? Having fallen in love with the man of my life?)

"How could you behave like this? Sleeping with someone you barely knew!"

(This is what human beings generally call love)

"And doing this to your parents, who are such good Catholics, true believers!"

(I beg your pardon, I am a woman of deep faith too)

He stopped for a couple of seconds. I could still recognize his seasoned theatrical art even in such a humiliating situation. To be fair to him, he had always been the best preacher of the monastery. I knew his high-pitched voice would now move up to a dramatic tone and attain its climax.

"And how could you forget about the terrible image of Sicily you were projecting in a foreign country?"

(Are you serious? Compared to mafia crimes and corruption?)

"Can't you see the evil that you have spread and that will cause terrible sufferings to so many other Sicilian girls, raised in the respect of religious precepts?"

(Now it's me who am speechless. I had no idea of the extent of my power)

"You did not have the right!"

He stopped short of pounding his fist on the table. He did not need to. He had incorporated the same amount of violence into his look and tone. I felt truly humiliated. I knew I did not deserve any of his poisonous arrows, and I would have loved to be able to throw back at him even a tenth of all the intelligent, sarcastic, and contemptuous replies that were rushing to my head (some of which I have put in italics above) as he shoved his violent accusations at me. Alas, nothing would emerge from my inner emotional Big Bang. I remained there, frozen like a deer in car headlights, my breath suspended. He continued in the same tone for some time, while my memory was busy bringing to mind similar scenes where my father would angrily shout at me that I was wrong: how could I be so stupid, where had all my intelligence gone, and so on and so forth. I did not know at the time that incidents of this sort populate an entire field of psychology and that there are ways to address them skillfully, namely through self-compassion. All I could feel was a hail of bullets tearing through my heart, some fired by the man in front of me, some hitting me from past memories.

I was out of breath. It felt like my chest was shrinking. However, I still managed to politely tell him goodbye—in a very low voice—at the end of his show. When I finally got out into the huge courtyard of the shrine, shaded by majestic chestnut trees, I started weeping with rage. Yes, I had denied a voice to my anger, partly because the only acceptable way to react to violence for a good and respectable girl was to act as if it had never happened, and partly because I did not want to leave behind any trace of the scathing humiliation he had inflicted on me. I still had some pride left. Not sure that was the optimal reaction, but it was the only one I had ever been allowed to practice.

Finding refuge in Serge's arms was the best remedy for that appalling encounter. Today that conversation would go very differently for sure; but this harrowing experience taught me a lot about what I would not accept from authoritarian people any more. It also started clearing the way for humility to become a pillar of my inner freedom.

✳ ✳ ✳

The same bitter taste of humiliation resurfaced many, many years later, when a disturbing miscommunication incident with my superior helped me understand even better the relationship between power and humility.

Robert, my boss at that time, was the chair of a panel in charge of selecting the candidates for the post of deputy manager in my unit. As the manager in charge, I was also a member of the panel, together with Sandra, a very knowledgeable senior adviser in our policy field. We had preselected four candidates, three women and a man, based on their resumes and motivation letters. I had a personal preference for one of the candidates; she was the most promising leader emerging in my team, but I was not opposed to considering other outstanding candidates.

However, in the days prior to the interviews something troubling happened. One of the other candidates, Camila, started calling several people in my unit, including me. I felt the calls, and in particular her reaching out to me, as attempts to impress all of us with her upscale resume (she had been working with one of the most powerful top managers in the Commission), as well as an easy way of learning what she should have been researching on our website and studying on her own, as the other candidates were surely doing. In particular, I distinctly perceived her questions as a dishonest way of finding out what we were going to ask at the interview.

The day of the interviews came, and we proceeded to ask the same questions to the four candidates, as required by the set procedure. Camila was very good in what she replied. I noticed, however, her tendency to emphasize her excellent relationship with the powerful boss she was serving, and to hint more at the political importance of what she was currently doing than at what she would work on in my team, if appointed. This confirmed my gut feeling that she had no real interest in our policy area and basically only wanted the promotion. I decided not to speak first once she left, to see whether my impressions were shared by the others. Sandra took the floor and expressed, in a very factual way, exactly what I had observed. I agreed with her and reinforced her views.

My boss clearly did not like our remarks, and took them as a slap in the face. It emerged that he had really appreciated Camila's performance. He got angry and started accusing us of being unfair to the lady, just because she was coming from outside the unit, even wondering whether we had not conspired to combine our efforts to favor the internal candidates.

His heated words did not land well with me. I was sensing there was something wrong in the entire situation. I chose to request a meeting with him, explaining that I had some points I wanted to bring to his attention before we decided on the two candidates to go forward—the final decision belonging to the head of our department. He agreed to meet me online. My heart was pounding as I clicked on the Skype link to reach him. I knew this conversation could go very wrong. However, I considered it my duty to disclose finally the questionable behavior Camila had displayed before the interview.

What I had not anticipated at all was that Robert would become mad at me, calling my attitude "bitchy" and criticizing me bitterly. He went on and on about my being unfair to a poor colleague who was just trying to show her talents, who in his view had been the best candidate so far, and would certainly make a great deputy for me. I tried to insist that Sandra, too, shared my views, and there he practically started shouting that Sandra's behavior was unacceptable, that she was being nasty to Camila only because she could not remain objective in front of such a talented, nice, and well-spoken candidate.

I could feel how my body was reacting. I felt my throat shrink and my guts sink; a rush of powerless anger drew tears to my eyes. It had been a long time since I felt so mistreated. I had felt compelled to share my perception of Camila's behavior before the interview with an open heart, convinced that he would understand what I meant, or at least listen to me. No assumption could have been more wrong. He was becoming more furious every second at what he termed "an anti-Camila conspiracy", in spite of my attempts to calm him down by repeating that I would of course accept whatever decision he would take. It was difficult to bring such a dramatic discussion to an undramatic close, and it took me over two weeks to start envisaging that I could ever speak to him again.

Just for you to know, in the end Camila withdrew her application and the head of the department appointed my preferred candidate to the post. I was totally relieved, and I decided that I had to draw all possible lessons from what had happened. I was not ready to go through such an upsetting experience again!

Soon after, through meditation and self-reflective exercises, I was able to identify the red thread connecting that confrontation with my boss and my humiliation by Father Tommaso, and, even further up the stream of my life, with the stern authority exerted on me by my father. But neither the priest nor Robert was my father, and in any case I was a grown-up now.

I had never forgotten the insulting accusations thrown at me by Father Tommaso, and for this reason I never agreed to see him again, in spite of regular attempts made by my mother to arrange a further meeting. But this time the predicament I was finding myself in had a different spin. I could imagine that my boss was striving to do his best, treat male and female colleagues the same way, and control his sudden anger surges. Moreover, I had to be professional and find a practical way out, because I had to continue working with him; a radical decision, like I had chosen in relation to Father Tommaso, was a no-go.

Mental association brought to mind some very tough discussions with my father. These revolved around the fact that my father considered make-up and miniskirts off-limits for me, and every single evening I had out of the house required long and unnerving discussions, as we were coming from often opposite understandings of life. Sometimes I lost, and spent my evenings writing melancholic poems in my bedroom, which often looked forward to my liberating departure from home. On some occasions I obtained the permission to go out, but at the cost of severe curfew hours—indeed, I was used to the word *coprifuoco* (curfew in Italian) in my life well before the pandemic. It could also happen that he would look at me (to be honest, mostly he tried to avoid the dreaded encounter with my heavy make-up and minimalistic miniskirts) just before going out and shout at me until I washed my face and changed my outfit. This just meant that I would put on my make-up (and sometimes the forbidden skirt) in the car of the friends picking me up. An omen of something I was confronted with later as a manager: bosses need to nudge their staff to follow instructions, because they cannot force anything onto unwilling employees.

However, I knew that conflicts between progressive girls and conservative parents were more than normal, and actually they had taught me the essentials of diplomacy and the power of good negotiation. Similarly, what could conflicts with my boss teach me about relationships at work? My Coach Number One had often observed that I had the unfortunate tendency to relate to my bosses as if they were my father, and this deserved reflection. Almost unconditional love was the driving force behind my father's behavior, the "almost" meaning that he would get angry whenever he saw how imperfect I was in relation to his belief system. This demanded that girls fall short only of the Virgin Mary—no way could we conceive a baby without sexual intercourse, that much he could concede. The consequence of this being that he persistently tried to make me perfect in the way he conceived perfection, an endeavor doomed to fail for any parent.

In the case of Robert—like other superiors that preceded him—it was not about perfection. It was the unspoken assumption that, if you have authority over somebody else in a professional setting, your opinions are by nature more worthy than theirs, and that person, being subordinate to you, has to agree that you are right. I had found the worm in the apple! Of course, I had to do what the boss decided, unless that was unethical or otherwise illegal. But the boss had no right to assume that his view of things was by nature better or fairer than mine. I had unexpectedly found common ground with all the human beings opposing excessive, authoritarian, or absolute power. But I was still unaware of the quality that could completely free me from any form of submission to sheer power. My experience taught me that this quality was humility.

Many, if not most, of the people I know (including me) have been brought up with the conviction that being humble means realizing and feeling that we are not better or more than the others. Simple and clear.

However, when we go deeper into humility—as I have done since I started my journey into compassion—at some point we realize that this definition of humility is incomplete, because it lacks its symmetric other part: we are not worse than anybody else either. Actually, being truly humble means knowing, and feeling, that we are neither above nor beneath anyone. That means that I am no better, humanly, existentially, and spiritually speaking, than, for example, the homeless person asking for money in the underground station. I am no more than them by nature. But I am no less a person either than the most acclaimed writers or Hollywood stars—let alone colleagues who have been promoted to higher positions than mine in my organization.

An aha moment! How liberating! How on earth could I live more than half a century without realizing this profound truth?

For the sake of precision, this enlightenment came to me in March 2021, after digesting a wonderful Applied Compassion Training lesson, explaining why humility is one of the pillars of compassion. *Humus* means soil, ground, in Latin: humility keeps us close to the ground, to reality, to nature, to everything and everybody else—and well-grounded where we belong and where we will return. Like everyone else. Not more, not less. Humility reflects the fact that we all share the same common humanity. As a matter of fact, we share 99,99% of our genetic material. But humility also reflects that we are all different, and unique, because each of us is the evolving result of unique circumstances and coincidences, heritage and personal traits, time and space. Therefore, each of us holds infinite worth.

So, what can humility do in the face of power? First of all, not being impressed by it. Second, replying assertively. Third, knowing that no power can deprive us of our intrinsic human dignity, even in the extreme case where it deprives us of our life. Fancy a concrete example? Take Jesus standing tall in front of Pontius Pilate. Bear with me if you have no familiarity with the Gospel, I will try to walk you through the scene, so that you can see it too.

Here comes Jesus, hurt, suffering, in pain and blood. The world has just turned upside down for him. One week earlier he had been acclaimed by the local population as he entered Jerusalem, everybody saluting him and honoring his name. On the following Friday, having spent a sleepless night where he sweated blood, knowing that his violent—and undeserved—end of life is closing in on him, that he has been betrayed by his best friends and accused of high crimes, he is dragged in front of the most powerful man in his geo-political world: the Roman Governor of Judea. Just to feel the thrill, imagine being dragged in front of, say, the big boss of the Guantanamo Bay detention camp. Basically you know that your life is in their hands, and a word spoken by you could cost you hurt, pain, possibly death. How would you feel? Frankly, I would give everything not to be put in such a position. Let's not even dwell on the fact that Jesus could have escaped to Egypt or somewhere else because he had seen all of this coming. He knew it, otherwise what's the point of being the Son of God? He chose to stay.

And now that he is facing Pilate, how does he behave? First, he remains silent. By now we are all congratulating him on this wise choice of shutting up and hoping that the dreadful moment goes away. A miracle can always happen! So, we are all there, rooting for him, because even if we don't believe that he is the Son of God we know he is innocent. If he has never hurt anyone, why arrest him, let alone sentence him to death? Things start looking brighter for him, as Pilate can't be forced to believe that he is a real threat to the Roman Empire. Then, when he has almost made it, he starts replying to Pilate. Oh my goodness! What happened? Has he just gone mad? Why on earth start to address the most powerful man in the region, the one appointed by the Emperor himself, who can decide in a breath to take his life?

Yet, he speaks. And he speaks from a place of humility, telling him, the Roman Governor, that if he had been born to become a king in this world, his troops would have defended him. Even a child would realize that—but, come on, who would dare speak the truth to such a powerful man? Especially if dragged in chains in front of him! And he continues calmly, explaining that his kingdom is of a different nature. Great sharing, you must be thinking now, but most of us would have saved it for a more appropriate venue and audience.

No, I am not trying to bring *Life of Brian* to the next level. I am just trying to describe the humility of Jesus in a situation where very few would have behaved in a similar way. I am neither a heroine nor a martyr. However, since the moment humility really started to sink into me I have kept less silent in front of my own Pontius Pilates. I have responded to humiliation more skillfully than with Father Tommaso or Robert. I have learned to stand my ground politely but firmly. To respect the line of command without giving up on an independent mind. And I have freed my working relationships from the enslaving grip of power dynamics.

Pinuccia Contino

***

An even more wondrous discovery of mine was that humility is not necessarily an antidote to power, or a way to oppose it. Humility can also inhabit power. We are not very used to real life examples of people exerting their power in a humble way, especially at work or in politics, so when we stumble upon one we generally marvel at it. But it is totally possible. It may even happen in our life.

I have experienced managerial power from both sides at work. For around two decades I have been a manager, therefore a boss to my team members too. I have always striven to be good and fair to my colleagues. But I am obviously not perfect, and I am aware I have improved a lot over time—which inevitably means that I have made mistakes.

Let me swallow my pride here, and confess that this is still difficult for me to accept. Sure, being present and aware has become my path to seeing my mistakes more clearly, little by little. Luckily my strong sense of justice has worked like a litmus test for me: whenever my error is not just due to factual circumstances, like forgetting something or making an awkward bodily movement, but is the result of a conscious choice on my part, I tend to recognize it and feel sorry for it: I admit I could have chosen to express more love and compassion toward others. Regret leads me to apologize and correct my mistake if possible.

When I say justice, I have in mind its empowering meaning. To me, justice happens when we experience the freedom to be who we truly are. Injustice, therefore, is anything that sits in the way and does not allow us to be who we are. But as we can only change what we have the power to impact on, I have decided to work on my perceptions, habits, and boundaries in order to grow justice in my life and around me.

To illustrate this, let me share here two very different experiences with power, humility, and justice that I went through as a boss. I'll start with a negative experience that left a bitter taste in my mouth and damaged a very positive working relationship that had started with my enthusiastic hiring of a very promising candidate, Roman. A story that exemplifies how a wrong choice coming from insufficient love and courage led me to increase injustice at work.

Roman was a competent, dynamic, effective, and quick colleague whom I had picked for one of the first teams I led. Extremely pleased with my choice, I had decided to entrust the most important project of the unit to him and Agata, another equally brilliant recruit of mine. They ran with it, and managed to forge lasting bonds with the rest of the team. As Agata, the strategic mind of the unit, used to put it, Roman was a doer. He would leave no deadline unkept, no action unfinished, no to-do-list unticked. As a junior and inspired manager myself, I brimmed with pride when looking at my outstanding crew.

This idyllic journey came to an abrupt end a couple of years later, when a total reorganization of the department resulted in the dismantlement of my team, dubbed "the miracle unit" by colleagues in human resources, and glued bits and pieces of it together with other bits, torn away from less miraculous teams, to set up the new team I was called upon to lead. Under these adverse circumstances, I had no choice but to pair Roman with Philippe, a troubled colleague, much older than him, who had a lot on his private life plate and was not the easiest man to work with. Roman asked me for help several times, explaining that he could not sleep at night, forever ruminating on the difficulties he encountered daily in working with Philippe, and feeling powerless to solve them. I knew very well that Philippe displayed excessive authority when talking, often humiliating his younger and brighter colleague, while lacking follow-through and consistency when it was necessary to act, thus leaving the entire work burden on Roman while giving him no recognition for his efforts. I realized that Roman must have been really suffering by the time he put his pride aside and revealed his struggle to me.

The problem was that I found myself in the midst of an inner storm due to the reorganization. I was feeling anxious for my future, insecure, and defensive. I felt unable to address the thorny problem of my colleagues' working relationship and I simply gave up. I was honest enough to tell Roman that I had no strength left to deal with the issue, and left him to his own devices. But honesty is not a magic wand. I later realized that Roman must have felt completely let down by me and deeply disappointed by my inability to even start addressing the issue. My sense of justice made me feel very sad and guilty over this. I clearly missed a great opportunity to love my colleagues more, to be brave enough to propose a solution and decrease their suffering.

For years after we both changed jobs, every time I tried to approach Roman to make amends, he never let me explain or apologize. I cannot blame him for distancing himself from me. It was my job and my responsibility at least to try and find a way out. For a long time, it was difficult for me to let go and accept his rejection. Now I have come to terms with this black spot in my career as a boss. I have let go completely of the hope that one day Roman may finally forgive me for the suffering that I caused to him. Have I forgiven myself for not being the perfect manager I wanted to be? I think so. I am not perfect, and even if I strive not to make mistakes I cannot get it right in every situation.

This experience also taught me the difference between shame and guilt. When you feel guilty, you can forgive yourself, because it is all about behavior. When you feel ashamed, you have a different kind of nut to crack, because the problem is not just about isolated acts, choices, or decisions. The problem is that you feel you are wrong, or not enough. That happens to be an area reserved for bodily appearance in my life. But that deserves a chapter, n° 9, for itself.

Let us turn now to the other episode. This time, contrary to what happened with Roman, it started badly and ended on a high note, which meant redemption—and much more—to me.

Let's travel backward in time for a decade or so. At the beginning of the year I was welcoming Angela back to the team. She had taken a career break and for a couple of years had mainly taken care of her kids and studied painting. Knowing that she had a bright mind and was a very dependable colleague, I offered her the challenge of coordinating one of the most important international events we were organizing. I was sure this would motivate her greatly, and help her return smoothly to the unit. Angela enthusiastically accepted and eagerly dove into the numerous tasks needed to build up a successful conference. However, after a couple of months on the file, she started showing signs of nervousness, sometimes developing into a sense of feeling overwhelmed. She was a very private person, so she rarely complained or shared the difficulties she was going through with colleagues. On my side, I was enjoying a peak of very innovative activities in the unit, and I interpreted these reactions as signs of her commitment and high professional standards.

Then came the twist. In June, she passed by my office and told me that she had not been sleeping for months. I could not believe my ears, as she had been putting up a brave face and carrying on as if everything was fine.

I did not know much about burnout in those days, nor was I trained to recognize its symptoms. This saved me from feeling guilty, without preventing me from doing the right thing. I immediately scaled down her workload, asking her to inform me as soon as she felt overwhelmed again. This happened intermittently over the following six months, making me fear that she would fall into the hole of a fully-fledged burnout. However, Angela never needed to take extended sickness leave, managed to work throughout the big conference, and obtained a promotion in the process.

I have always felt relatively neutral about this story, the surfacing of the problem, and the way I tackled it. I know I did my best, and the fact that I managed to preserve Angela's health as much as I could shielded me from feeling that I acted poorly as a manager. But the moment that I will always remember with surprise, thankfulness, and joy happened years later. Angela and I had volunteered to lead a walk together for colleagues coming back to work from burnout in the Tournay-Solvay Park, a gorgeous patch of greenery on the southern edge of Brussels. At some point, after listening to the moving experiences shared by the participants, she caught up with me on the path into the forest and stated, "Pinuccia, I want to thank you for the way you reacted to my burnout when we were working together."

"Why thank me, Angela? I am sorry I did not know anything about it back then. I just tried to do my best."

"No, you did much more. I have just realized it, listening to the burnout stories of the colleagues. I could have had a different boss, insensitive or too busy to notice and act, like them. You are different: you did care for me."

Tears are coming to my eyes while I am transcribing her words, as they still resonate in my memory. For quite some years already I have learned to accept gratitude with gratitude, but I was not expecting that exchange at that point in time. Angela gave me a wonderful gift that day, as she basically expressed the belief that I had made a difference in her life. And, as small as that difference might be, I realized right then that this was what I had been craving for so long, more than anything else: to have a positive impact on as many people as I could. To develop my way to exert power in the direction of service and love. To bring about more justice. Certainly not the usual "career plan" at work!

Humility became my biggest ally. Day after day, it helped me develop more skillful responses to hurtful behaviors displayed by my bosses. It also taught me how to become a better boss myself. That's what made the difference between my relationship with Roman compared to my relationship with Angela. Without realizing it yet, I was deconstructing the mainstream culture of success, and experiencing humility as a fundamental component of power when it contains compassion.

No wonder humility has consistently showed up in my life as a catalyst for justice, in the sense that every time I have been able to act from a place of humility, I have increased the chances for justice to flourish, like in the story of Angela. The same happens every time I don't cover up something that I don't know, and, instead of sweeping my ignorance under the rug, I ask the experts in my team how they would approach it. The result is inevitably more effective and impactful. And it feels much more like success than any formal title or official role to me.

To sum up, my experience of power relationships in the workplace has involved suffering every time I felt humiliated by my boss or I realized I could have been a better manager to colleagues working with me. The humiliation I felt as a result of the exertion of hierarchical or authoritarian power on me, whether at work or in more personal contexts like church and family, was due to the fact that I was accepting to play with the usual rules of the game, including domination and submission, and not practicing humility enough. In this way I was still granting power to others with a bigger role or title than mine to dominate or crush me. As soon as I realized that humility actually liberates us from the need to obtain validation, recognition, or promotion from others, and therefore from their power over us, I felt a growing sense of freedom. I gave myself permission to feel as a human being who is no better and no worse than anybody else. To put my relationships, including at work, in a different context; to choose not the power to rule others, but the power to serve them as a peer who has decided to do so from a place of humility. And that increased justice, meaning the freedom to be who we are, in my life and in the life of those around me.

To summarize and help you practice, through meditation, journaling, or self-reflection, I have listed here the self-inquiry questions underpinning chapter 4:

- If I repeat to myself "I am above and below no one", what do I feel in my body? What sensations, feelings, emotions arise?
- Can I find an example of how I manifested humility in a work situation?
- Can I bring to mind a situation where I did not behave in a way I consider adequate? What emotions does this memory bring up and where do I feel them in my body?
- Can I explore what justice means to me? Can I connect a recent experience at work with my sense of justice? How did that situation feel in my body?
- Can I bring to mind a situation where my behavior increased (or decreased) justice at work? What could I have done differently? What teachings can I distil from that situation?

And you can add your own self-inquiry questions below:

_____
_____
_____
_____
_____

Finally, I have selected a resource for you that I find very powerful in connection with this chapter, an extraordinary TEDx talk on the power of humility by Dr Ernest Fokoue:
https://www.youtube.com/watch?v=D6FnZtfo9As

For more, don't hesitate to browse through my "Recommended Resources" at the end of the book.

CHAPTER FIVE

Vulnerability, the Unassuming Strength

Shake It Out, Florence and the Machine

Toward the end of my 30s I would describe myself as a happy wife, a proud mother of three, and a successful aide to a European Commissioner—who is equivalent, to a certain extent, to a minister but at the European level. There were moments I felt like I was in heaven: the bliss could range from sharing a delicious meal to celebrate Serge's birthday to, as you may remember, shaking hands with the Dalai Lama. My children running into my arms after singing nursery rhymes and top hits from my youth together brought tears of joy to my eyes, and choosing the model and shape of my new, bright blue, obviously Italian kitchen made me feel n° 1 in interior design.

Most of the time, however, I dragged myself to the office and back, feeling miserable and irritated.

The truth was that I was getting more and more impatient to climb the next step on the career ladder. At that time, statistics showed that generally European civil servants became managers in their early forties. With my usual self-confidence, by the age of 35 I reckoned that I was fully apt to manage the policies I was an expert in—education, research, and languages—and lead a team of 10 to 20 people. From that moment on, I kept very busy comparing every aspect of my professional life with those of my colleagues who were more or less in the same age, career, and competence brackets and were little by little being promoted to managerial positions. I compared experience, salary level, time spent in the different sectors and functions, proximity to power, intelligence, strategic vision, public speaking skills, number of languages spoken, and I am certainly forgetting many others. Looking at the progress of others I started to feel stuck in my prestigious, but temporary, member-of-cabinet function.

This reflex was relatively new in my life. During my childhood and adolescence, my passion for learning, coupled with the principle I upheld to always help everybody else in class, had shielded me from these kinds of reflections. I was too busy explaining philosophy lessons and letting my school mates copy my answers to mathematics problems and Latin—or ancient Greek—exercises.

When I succeeded in three open competitions to become a European civil servant, which have always attracted tens of thousands of brilliant graduates from all over Europe, I was still bathing in the blissful mindset of somebody who has nothing to prove because everything comes naturally to them. What other proof of professional achievement could I possibly need? Becoming a lifelong European official and being able to serve the noble European ideal as a member of its high-performing multicultural administration appeared to me as the logical response to my ambition in my mid-twenties.

It certainly was, and it did happen. But it marked also the start of a whole new phase in my life, where work (and family) would acquire a deeper meaning and require skills whose existence I was then barely aware of.

One of the skills I lacked was the ability to reply promptly and wittily to statements which I perceived as offensive. For example, in the early 90s, mundane jokes often reflected biased judgments. Indeed, many people thought that they were being funny when having this conversation with me:

"Where do you come from?"

"Catania."

Mentioning my city of origin was usually followed by:

"And where is that?" to which I would reply, "In Sicily," politely omitting a heartfelt "you ignoramus".

That was the moment they would carelessly fire back: "Ah! Mafia!"

As if that were the cleverest, most impressive and meaningful way to start a conversation with a gentle, smart, and well-intentioned young stranger! On those occasions I would experience an immediate surge of confused inner protests and possible rebuttals. The confusion stopped me from ever delivering the defining retort, the one to be remembered forever by my interlocutors, an incendiary reply that would stop the mafia reference in its tracks once and for all.

Pinuccia Contino

If that reference used to make me freeze it was probably due to the fact that it lit up a much more ancient and hurtful memory, something that had happened when I was five years old. You may remember that in those distant years we were living in the suburbs of Milan, because my father had accepted a transfer to Northern Italy to get a promotion. We lived not far from Switzerland, where products like cigarettes and chocolate were much cheaper than in Italy, so we used to drive regularly up to Lugano. I had just learned to read and this was opening up a new universe to me. I was eager to decipher anything written that fell under my eyes, be it detergent labels or opening times glued to restaurant doors. Lugano is situated in the Italian-speaking part of Switzerland, so for me it was a great joy to walk around a city abroad (the first foreign city I ever visited) and be able to understand whatever written word combination met my eyes. So, I was really astonished when I read the following sentence on one, two, and then several restaurant and bar entrances: *Vietato entrare ai cani e ai meridionali* (no dogs or Southerners allowed).

Besides my child's reflection that Swiss people must really be stupid if they believed that dogs could actually read—and thus politely refrain from entering—the widespread, ominous prohibition left me with a lot of question marks. Why would people from the South of Italy (this is what *meridionali* means in my mother tongue) not be allowed to enter public places like bars and restaurants? What were we guilty of? OK, maybe dogs could be dirty and bark too loudly, but I knew plenty of Southerners and they were all clean and well-behaved people ...

As generally happens in such cases, I turned to my parents, who shrugged and sadly replied that this was a sign of racism. I inquired about the meaning of this new word and they explained that people who wrote such things believed that we were bad because we came from a poor area of Italy. Of course, that was not true (that we were bad) and it was not our fault (that we were poor), but we could not do much to change their views. By the way, Germans were well known for being racist against Italians from the South too, as my aunt and uncle often pointed out after they moved close to Stuttgart to work in a firm subcontracting to Mercedes. My parents concluded that the best thing to do was to avoid entering those places.

As a five-year old child, I thought I could easily follow their recommendation. It was too early for me to understand that discrimination is not confined to places where it is explicitly said that you are not welcome or allowed in. It took me years to understand that discrimination is part and parcel of our human experience, including at work. And that the place where we can overcome it is our heart, where humility can make us feel grounded in our infinite value as unique human beings. Whatever others may think of us. From that moment on, we can also learn to befriend our vulnerability. Even to adopt it as a shortcut to courage. This helps us and everybody around us see the world differently.

Including when considering career prospects.

※ ※ ※

Going back to the time I served in cabinets, as I said, I was impatient to become a manager. My ambition had taken a new turn, compared with my behavior as a pupil, a student, and a junior civil servant, maybe unconsciously reacting to memories of racist or discriminatory behaviors I had suffered. For as long as I was studying, I used to perform at my highest level first and foremost because I loved learning, not because I wanted to stand out compared to others. However, after over a decade of professional life, the expectation that you needed to "beat your competition" in the race for managerial jobs to demonstrate your value had rubbed off on me.

Being a manager in a high-performing, politically complex, and multicultural setting like the European Commission entails rushing around handling something like 40 different cases, 30 urgencies, 20 people, and 10 conflicting priorities at the same time, every day of the year. Quite a sporting accomplishment! And for sure, the hyper-active and super-human persona generally associated with being a highly performing manager has scared off more than one colleague, and particularly women. But, to me, landing one of these jobs meant getting the recognition I needed and felt like an appealing endeavor.

I certainly wished to lead a team empathically and have a bigger impact on the world. In other words, before I even knew the research and the data that supports it, I was already cultivating compassionate leadership. Compassionate leadership means leading both yourself and others with compassion for a compassionate purpose, creating a work culture that supports everyone's thriving and growing. "Leading for compassion with compassion", as my teachers Laura Berland and Evan Harrel define compassionate leadership in their training courses. My experience of teamwork had showed me that I could lead people to work well together, performing and thriving. That I could multiply each individual's impact to make Europe an even better place to live in. But my ambition was also rooted in the need to be recognized for my real value, a way to prove all those who had been dismissive against me wrong.

I had to take part in three different selection procedures in succession over three years to become a manager. I started when my third and last child turned two, probably because I then felt finally free to hunt for the promotion and the demanding job I longed for. It was painful. I jumped, fell to the ground and got back on my feet twice. When I tried for the third time, I promised to myself it would be the last, whatever happened. I applied only in policy areas that really motivated me, even if I could have gone for more simply to get the promotion. But the discomfort that I had felt going through the motions of the selection process had been so upsetting at times that in my mind it was starting to offset all the positive sides of being given an official mandate to manage a team.

My promotion to a managerial role finally solved the conundrum. I looked on this achievement as the official confirmation that I had what it took to be an excellent manager, and that I was ripe for the challenge at an age which was perfectly aligned with the norm! I was so excited that I felt goosebumps and butterflies in my stomach every time I pictured my first day as a manager. Daniel, my future principal, had phoned me to announce that he had chosen me for the job because there was fire in me, as he expressively put it, describing my passionate performance at the interview. However, for different reasons, three months passed between that call and the moment I took up my new responsibilities. That gave me ample time to prepare for my much-coveted new professional challenge.

I had been appointed manager of the unit dealing with language policy in one of our biggest departments. I was arriving at the right moment.

Daniel was highly cultivated, passionate about languages, and had just got the opportunity to give a political boost to language learning in Europe. His idea was to improve the way languages and translation were taught at European universities so that students could get better jobs. He had the language experts, the vision, and now even the right manager for this: I had been dealing with language policy for several years in the cabinet, so much so that I was dubbed "Madame Multilingualism". I knew where we were coming from in political terms and how to develop a policy through projects, awards, and networks. He was also convinced that I would be able to motivate and empower my staff on this journey.

In spite of a difficult start with him when I joined the cabinet, due to our sometimes different visions of political priorities, our working relationship had evolved positively. He quickly realized that I would not shy away from defending the resources of his department if anyone attempted to deplete it to the advantage of higher-profile policies. I was loyal to my professional role and this loyalty was strongly rooted in my personal values. I have always believed that one of the prerequisites of democracy is for the law to speak the language of the citizens it addresses. I had always been passionate about languages, first and foremost because good communication across cultures is more likely to happen when we talk the same language.

Daniel possessed a strategic view of the role of languages in the world and believed in people with talent and courage. When I phoned him to ask whether he would be open to consider my application for the job so as to check his reaction, he immediately replied, "It would be an honor for me if you were to apply for this position." I could not believe my ears, and certainly this exchange has earned its place among my most precious professional memories. I will always be grateful to him for having believed in me and for bringing me into a new dimension of my career.

We had a good discussion to prepare my arrival in the unit and the mandate he gave me then was very clear: he needed both my guts and my wit to launch the first network of universities offering the best Master degrees in translation across Europe. This project was a long-standing idea that had never bloomed into a fully-fledged network. Interestingly enough, it had become hostage to a select group of highly-reputed university professors who appeared to be never satisfied with the strategy to follow, the selection criteria, nor the governance arrangements to be set up to ensure that the network would be both sustainable and able to inspire excellence in other university programs.

I was brimming with energy, strategies, and plans, and he knew I would not waste a second to start the ball rolling. Daniel recommended that I be as diplomatic as possible with those hardcore academics to avoid a mutiny, as their academic prestige was the guarantee of the future network's excellence. So, the day I took up my managerial duties I immediately talked with the team, breathing into my colleagues all the passion and energy that I possessed, and discussing with them the strategy I had imagined for fulfilling my mission. We shared out among ourselves the phone calls to the famous professors. Two of these were French and I reserved them for myself, as I had heard they were the tough cookies.

I felt very proud, also considering the reactions of my new team: relief, enthusiasm, admiration. I thought I had covered every aspect and anticipated every risk. Until, ten days later, I got my first cold shower as a manager.

I had just received an email from Daniel's secretariat, asking me to prepare a reply to a letter attached to the message. The letter was signed by one of the French professors I had spoken to in the name of the entire core group. It listed all the dangers that my "unrealistic" ideas to "rush" the project to completion would create for the very concept of excellence in translation.

I felt a rush of adrenaline and my first thought was, "How can they be so stupid? Didn't they realize that I would be asked to prepare the reply to this letter?" However, just moments afterward, the ebb of my energy left me in near-despair: how could I be so unlucky? I did not deserve such mistrust! I had been doing everything by the book, talking to them personally, keeping them at the heart of the project, already announcing that they would be part of the selection committee, entrusted with vetting the selection criteria and the application form. I had been honest and transparent, explaining why compelling political reasons demanded that the selection be carried out, and the network up and running, by the end of the year.

After the desolation, though, came fury. These academics did not have the slightest idea of how a policy project was run! That's why they had been dragging on and on, never able to propose something clear, precise, and feasible! Neither had they met among my predecessors a counterpart who could stand up to their fame and impressive resumes, have the courage to express a different view, and act accordingly.

What It Takes to Be Yourself

One of my favorite T-shirts (my photo)

No guts, no glory. I had always liked the saying, mainly because of how crisp and well-cut it sounded. I finally understood in my body what that motto meant.

I went to see my big boss, who started the meeting with a good laugh.

"So, do you already have a draft reply for my signature?"

He knew me better than what I thought! I explained the polite point-by-point rebuttal I was going to draft, with a conclusion that would be both firm and inclusive. Even if I did not appreciate their low blow, I knew they were the best European academics in translation studies, and I had to keep them on board for the good of the project.

Daniel approved my proposal with the expression of a satisfied cat. He signed the letter I prepared for him without delay and the professors understood that they had no choice other than to work constructively with me. So started a period of four years during which I developed a very strong relationship of mutual appreciation with them, managing to build together a European network of excellence in translation. A network which is still a beacon of multilingualism in Europe, and today embraces five times more members than at its start. As in my wildest dreams.

For the first time in my life, I felt I had become part of an awesome international community that spanned administration and academia. I felt on an equal footing with its members, who had outstanding talent and competences, and were ready to volunteer to improve the training and the job prospects of their students, preserve diversity, and allow Europe to grow without giving up on its cultural wealth.

I remember an occasion when some of "my professors", as I nicknamed them in my mind, jokingly complained in front of me to a newcomer, "Pinuccia is a tough cookie. She even manages to have us work for free." That was literally true, as I had no budget to reward their work for Europe. However, I was no slave master: each of them perfectly knew the priceless prestige that came with the network membership. And I am sure they loved working with me at least as much as I did with them. So much so that they brought tears to my eyes the day I bade farewell to the network by surprising me with a huge bouquet of roses and lilies.

Deep bows to all of you, my friends! Working with you and being accepted into your wonderful community was a real privilege and set a very high bar for the rest of my career.

※ ※ ※

As these busy and rewarding years went by, the awareness that my work could have more impact started building up inside me. That came with the feeling that I was good enough to apply for a further promotion. My best friends, too, deplored that my career was not taking off the way it could. In the hope of accelerating it, Silvia, one of my friends working in the Commission, offered to introduce me to her own principal, Claudia.

Silvia spoke of her as somebody "particularly gifted in the field of human resources."

"She is always interested in getting to know a competent manager because she is a woman of vision," trumpeted Silvia on the basis of her personal relationship with Claudia, who adored her. I took my friend at her word and accepted her generous offer.

I was aware that, as in every professional sector, introducing a friend to a VIP is risky business, because every side of the triangle has some stake in the game. In this case, Claudia wanted to please Silvia, who was one of her loyal allies. Silvia wanted to help me come out of a minor policy area lest I remained stuck there until my retirement. And I wanted to show up at my best to impress Claudia with what I believed were my undeniable professional credentials and what I considered to be the amazing achievements of my then 20-year-long career.

The much-awaited meeting was short and flavorless. It left me vaguely hopeful, but never led to any following step. Clearly Claudia did not share the enthusiasm I felt for myself, as I learned later from Silvia's lips, when I finally dared to ask what had happened in her view.

"She just commented, 'Who does this lady think she is? Nobody knows her.'"

Those few, reported words cut deep into my heart. The strong believer in myself that I had always been could not make sense of that pitiless judgment. Even my unshakeable belief in the fact that God loves me as I am was of no help here. No, understanding what had happened was of the essence. Why would the lady express such a radical judgment on me after a mere 15-minute-long conversation? The incident was offering me a unique opportunity to dive deeper and maybe learn something useful.

The prospect of learning had always cheered me up, even in the most somber circumstances. I therefore decided to ask Silvia for help, and started asking questions. The replies she gave me hurt, but started shedding some light on my predicament.

"Silvia, you have always told me that Claudia was an exemplary top manager. Why would she say something so mean about me?"

"Well, it's true that professionally you are not very visible."

My friend was right. I had never worked as a manager in one of the more "political" departments of the Commission. Language policy was not something you would find among the press scoops. This point was factual and clear.

Then something unexpected followed.

"The other thing is that you have always done what you wanted in your life. You have never sacrificed anything important for work—something that could show career really mattered to you."

Needless to say, I received those words, uttered by Silvia in a very light and self-evident tone, like arrows into my flesh. My mind started protesting that it was not true. I had worked countless hours and long days since I had joined the organization, I had demonstrated how good and effective I could be, and so on and so forth. But I stayed silent. I needed some quiet time to process the meaning of this unexpected feedback. In particular, what kind of sacrifices was she hinting at? What else could I do, apart from working hard and well? Had I failed somehow to show how much I was working? Or was I missing something bigger than that?

Like an ear bug, a suspicion started forming in my mind. I had never thought that I needed to do something special to prove to those who had the power to promote me that they could really trust me. In the case of Daniel, he had been clever and wise enough to infer this from my professional behavior and achievements. But maybe he was an exception, and I had mistaken the exception for the rule.

If you have watched "The Godfather" movies, you may remember that in order to be accepted into the "family", every newcomer needs to demonstrate their undisputable loyalty to the bosses. What if all power systems, in every human organization, worked the same way? The only difference being the kind of organization and the nature of the requirements. *Mutatis mutandis* (necessary changes made, pardon my Latin), what if I had little chance of being considered for higher positions because, very simply, I had not shown a strong enough grasp of power dynamics? After all, this was a very valid point for those who were in power.

Even worse, I had interpreted the usual narrative that merit was the most important element of a successful career the same way I did at school and university: study, perform, progress. I had naturally translated this into: work, perform, progress. Without understanding that "merit" at work is not as simple as a school grade. It is a much more complex concept and covers many more aspects. The criteria that paved the way to a successful career were numerous, and on several I scored only average, like in "putting my job before anything else", or even poorly, like when it came to networking.

The short encounter with Claudia was thus the starting point of a deep self-inquiry and long reflections on the roots of my professional ambition and what I needed to do for my career to evolve in the right direction.

※ ※ ※

In the last decade or so I tried several times to be promoted to the next career step and become a senior manager. In my organization, and I guess in many others, this involves a more complex selection procedure than the procedure to become a manager because it gives access to higher responsibilities. Every time I failed, I learned a bit more about the reasons behind the failure, and I continued trying. I hoped I would finally manage to be promoted, even though I knew there was no guarantee to succeed.

I learned a key lesson a couple of years ago, when I ran again for a senior management post. I had come to the decision to apply for several reasons. The job was a perfect fit for one of my own areas of expertise, consumer affairs. I could not imagine a more favorable opportunity, as I had worked in the area for several years and consumer policy had no more secrets for me. I also knew that many of my fellow managers would apply, plus several others from outside the department. It would have seemed weird that I did not. Last but not least, my team were my biggest cheerleaders. I did not want to disappoint them.

However, to me these procedures had become a real torment in terms of uncertainty, length, and possible humiliation stemming from comparison to others. A part of me was reluctant to join the race.

I spent the first month following my application for the post in a painful inner conflict that prevented me from starting to prepare for the interview. As a last resort, I knew I could withdraw my application at any point without needing to give a justification. Why on earth should I try again? Hadn't I already had my share of painful, humiliating, and unsuccessful procedures? Shouldn't I rather stand tall against the widespread view that becoming a senior manager was necessary to prove one's worth and professional success? Not for the sake of going counter the views of the majority (who couldn't care less about my inner struggles), but rather to be truthful to the person I had become. What was changing in my attitude compared with my previous attempts? Were the circumstances really that different? Of course, no two situations, even when similar, are ever the same in anyone's life, so this time I could hope for a better alignment of stars. However, if I had to take part in the race, my aim was to show up as a senior manager who would embody compassionate leadership.

On this point, several well-meaning and experienced colleagues, including Silvia, had advised me not to insist too much on compassion. They told me that not everybody understood the meaning of the word the way I meant it, that the role of a senior manager brought to mind strategy and effectiveness rather than decreasing suffering, that the interview panel needed to be reassured about the fact that I would not go off on some sort of New Age sidetrack, and so on.

Their recommendations did not surprise me, and this made me feel even less comfortable with the selection procedure. Because the only way I could imagine being a senior manager—and I knew I could be a great one, not only because I believed it sincerely but also because for years many colleagues had been wishing this for me—was to embody compassion even more and have more positive impact on my colleagues, on the organization, and on Europe. I did not feel like going into the interview as if I was going to an audition, faking a type of candidate the selection panel members were likely to be more comfortable with, but which I knew did not correspond to who I was.

So, after that painful period of inner conflict, I made the decision to run the race my way. And to state upfront that my biggest asset was compassion. I also prayed that in case I was not going to be appointed, my suffering could be shortened by an early exit from the race. Since I had already lived through a few selection procedures just to be discarded at the end, I really expressed that wish in full awareness.

This approach enabled me to prepare adequately and more peacefully for two months.

Then came the first interview, online. I believe I was good. Not perfect, of course. I was extremely tense and experienced some connection problems, but in my view I replied quite well to all questions. More importantly, I felt very aligned and authentic, because I did not shy away from mentioning compassion and why I felt this was absolutely needed for me to measure up to the new role if I were to be promoted.

Six weeks later I learned that I had not made it. I first got the news informally, via another candidate who had been admitted to the second phase of the selection procedure and wanted to know whether I too had been. At the beginning, when I received the bad news, I felt its full blow. Damn, it hurt! My body reacted as if I had the flu. I was feeling pain in my muscles, and that sort of relentless inner movement that makes one feel sick, a bit like vertigo.

I immediately decided to take a long, hot bath. That managed to calm me down and helped me take some distance from the news. I was convinced that compassion had been received with surprise and suspicion by some of the panel members and had negatively influenced my final ranking. But I did not spend any time venting against the situation, feeling pity for myself, or playing the movie of the interview over and over again. I did shed a couple of angry tears for the huge waste of energy those months had represented in my life. I had not even been able to salvage a minute to continue writing this book! I quickly realized that was my most bitter regret.

What did all this mean for my professional future? Was there a meaning, possibly hidden in plain view, for me to decipher in this—once again—sad experience?

I spent the following couple of days with my family and friends, and I watched *The Old Man* TV series starring Jeff Bridges. I often immerse myself in action movies or series when life becomes heavy on my shoulders, to occupy the ground of pain and give suffering less space to torment me.

And then, four days later, one of my senior managers, who was a member of the panel, came around to inform me officially. I had a fit of proud pleasure when I could answer his stumbling attempt to open the conversation on such a delicate topic like a big girl.

"Don't worry, I already know."

It was also a way to protect myself from *Schadenfreude*, to be perfectly honest. You know, the feeling that makes people rejoice when others get knocked out. But, in fact, from then on, the conversation flowed much more easily, as he was clearly relieved not to be the first one breaking the bad news to me. So, I could feel reassured and appreciate the fact that he had come to tell me this personally.

And, guess what, the very day I had the "official" conversation with my senior manager confirming that my race to the promotion ended there, I felt inspired to share the news with my unit. I explained to them that I had not made it. That of course it was not good news for me, but that the great gift in it was that I could continue being their boss, and that I really valued and cherished this prospect, because they were a wonderful team.

What happened just afterward took my breath away. They erupted in joyful cheers, saying that even though it was a shame, because I would have been a perfect fit for the job, they were all delighted that I would remain their manager. I was speechless, and felt like a wave of warmth coming my way. I would have liked to hug them all at the same time: their spontaneous expression of deep recognition for the value I brought to them and into the world made me feel both moved and amazed. Wasn't this the true essence of the success I had been craving? Did I really need a different title and a different job to be happy, while I was experiencing such a direct testimony of gratitude and appreciation from my entire team?

This single experience brought vulnerability into my leadership path well before I studied compassionate leadership, of which vulnerability is an attribute. Reflecting on what had happened, I realized that I had never shared a big failure with my entire team so openly. Sure, I happened to share some professional, or even personal, issues with individual colleagues, and I had become much more talkative on these than earlier on in my career, but I usually considered it not appropriate to expose my own problems to my 20 team members. I assumed they would be discouraged by my failures. If the boss couldn't put up a brave face against defeat, how would they manage their own? As if denying our fears and sorrows were ever helpful! As if faking indifference against the blows of life could decrease their impact on us!

What I felt that day deep inside me aligned with what I heard later in the podcasts and books on vulnerability and leadership by Brené Brown. That when we decide to share our disappointments, problems, and unmet needs with our co-workers, and we do it from a place of common humanity, in a way that allows them to see the learning points in those difficult experiences, we actually help them grow. We support them with our example. We show them that we can hold both failure and joy at the same time, if we only trust each other enough to share our troubles. Because we know that we are not perfect, and we know that we are stronger together. Always.

And you, how do you feel about vulnerability? Can you think of a situation in which you made a conscious choice to share something hard with your colleagues? And why did you do that? Just an honest self-inquiry, like a mirror would do. The mirror just reflects an image, it doesn't express any judgment, doesn't accuse, doesn't blame. This is the metaphor that my Stanford teachers, and more generally many mindfulness teachers, often use to insist on a non-judgmental attitude when we really want to approach an experience, a feeling, a situation in the most open and receptive way. You can jot down the most interesting points that emerge from your self-inquiry, and come back to them later to see if they can shed any further light on your questioning.

Since that day, I have become fully aware that what makes me truly happy at work has to do with who I am, not with who or what others think I should be. And that happiness is enhanced when people see me for real, and appreciate me because of that. Indeed, when I go deep inside myself, I do not find a desire for titles, jobs, or authority. I find a profound wish to help, create, and make a difference, which ultimately are expressions of love. It seems as if promotions lurked on my path to teach me that I did not truly need them, in spite of craving them for so long. That lesson went much further than my growing awareness of both the advantages I enjoyed and the disadvantages I suffered due to my personal, cultural, and socio-economic circumstances. Different types of experiences, often painful or difficult, like my Swiss memories and my learning curve as a manager, helped me develop a more balanced view of the whole and understand that success, in the sense of fulfilling our life purpose, is not a one-size-fits-all. Each of us needs to uncover it as we walk the path of life.

Moreover, fulfilling our life purpose is not something we obtain or conquer once and for all. It requires a journey into the mystery of our being that adds depth every time we peel a new layer off. So, the gift brought to me by my failure to get promoted was the awareness that I could be myself under any circumstances, including the most painful ones. That accepting and showing my vulnerability was actually a strength that inspired others, because it came from a place of humility and authenticity. That I could shake off corporate expectations just like I had learned not to be dependent on social perceptions, because the real treasure that attracted people to me and motivated them to give their best at work was not a title, a role, or a function.

It was my heart.

To summarize and help you practice, through meditation, journaling, or self-reflection, I have listed here the self-inquiry questions underpinning chapter 5:

- Can I connect with a situation where I felt discriminated against? How does that feel in my body? Is there a teaching for me to decipher in this experience?

- Do I need a different title and a different job to be happy? Can I explore what in my view would make me feel truly fulfilled? Can I think of a situation where I felt this way?

- What in my view is the true essence of the success I have been craving? Can I picture it in my mind, in all its details? How does that make me feel?

- How do I feel about vulnerability? Can I think of a situation in which I made a conscious choice to share something hard with my colleagues, family, loved ones, community members, or neighbors? And why did I do that?

- What is the real treasure that attracts people to me?

What It Takes to Be Yourself

And you can add your own self-inquiry questions below:

_____

_____

_____

_____

Finally, I have selected a resource for you that I find very powerful in connection with this chapter, Brené Brown's TED Talk on "The Power of Vulnerability":

https://www.youtube.com/watch?v=iCvmsMzlF7o

For more, don't hesitate to browse through my "Recommended Resources" at the end of the book.

CHAPTER SIX

Pride and Forgiveness

Hello, Adele

"What a tough cookie!"

This is certainly what Axel, the German guy I had been dating for six months by the end of 1989, must have thought the day I told him on the phone, "If you do not come to Sicily and visit me in January as you promised, just forget my phone number!"

I was 22 years old at that time, hopelessly romantic and dangerously prone to day-dreaming during the time left over from studying, dancing, writing poems, and chatting with my best friends on the phone. In the summer of 1989, when I set foot in Salamanca, the lovely Spanish city all dressed up in pink, orange, and yellow sandstone since the Middle Ages, I was more than ripe to fall crazily in love with the blond, blue-eyed, fit, and tall Teuton called Axel: the very embodiment of Prince Charming—what a dream for a Sicilian, brown-eyed, and curly brunette! For sure, I had never been so madly in love with anyone before. Many years later my

French friend Carole, whom I had met in Salamanca that same fateful summer, would suggest in her exquisite language that my love hormones appeared to reach a much higher level than his, and nobody would have bet a cent on our love story lasting until the end of the month, let alone six more months in distance mode. That was a time without smartphones and internet. No WhatsApp chats could fill the space and time between our weekly calls, which used to threaten me with tachycardia every time the phone would ring one or two minutes later than scheduled. Gone are those days, yet I still remember that period with affection and tenderness. I am guessing that you too have memories like this.

The love story with Axel and its abrupt ending did not come as a surprise to me. I could be incredibly devoted to my loved ones as a girlfriend, or even just as a friend; yet the moment a friend or boyfriend deceived me, I would turn the page on them without regret. Patricia, one of my favorite classmates in secondary school, might still happen to remember my first deed in this category. When I was 12, I managed not to address a word to her for eight long months because she had made fun of me during a volleyball game. I only agreed to speak with her again when she phoned me and asked for forgiveness. Today, I cannot believe I could be so stubborn and tough with people I was very fond of. And, as I grew up, I started displaying the same attitude toward the boys who had let me down. I clearly had an issue when it came to what I perceived as betrayal. The simple fact of being on the receiving end of what I read as a dismissive, humiliating, or otherwise deceptive behavior would completely block out any loving feeling for that person, and made me reject them 100%. In those early days, I basked in the conviction that it was a clear sign of strength.

Years later, similar emotions would inhabit me when it came to my career goals and hopes of advancement at work. Although it is something awkward to admit, what I went through when identifying an interesting job involving a further promotion would bring on a storm of feelings, a bit like a blossoming romance, as I prepared for the interviews, dreamed, and worried about the final result. So the time I got my biggest slap in the face in career terms my reaction reminded me astonishingly of my sudden dumping of Axel.

It happened in a very complicated year for me at the Commission. I was trying—again—to get promoted into the senior management level, at the same time I was caught in the whirlwind of a huge reorganization in my department, where I was leading the internal coordination team. So, I was happily and busily coordinating policy issues in different domains and thoroughly enjoying the creativity and energy of my team, when the decision to move me somewhere else as a consequence of the reorganization was dropped on me like a bomb.

I was certainly not delighted by my principal's decision, to say the least. However, I did not immediately realize the full weight of this blow—it was such an unwanted change—because at the same time I was in the throes of an intricate selection procedure to step up as a senior manager in a different department. Not once did I stop to reflect on the worrying fact that I had been taken unawares by the decision of my top management to move me to another post. I was still considering merit at face value, while, as in all complex organizations, the higher you aim, the more merit expands to include a strategic understanding of power dynamics and unflinching determination. My tendency to be an optimist against all odds did not help either.

The selection procedure was tough and excruciatingly long. I had started by approaching Lara, the head of the department in charge of event organization, when the vacancy was published. I had already learned at my own expense that sending in an application out of the blue was a doomed gesture. It was essential to signal your interest in the job when it was still possible to pick up any negative omens and withdraw the application if needed. During this first contact with her I heard only encouragements to apply, given "the relevance of my CV, my deep knowledge of the Union's policies, and my managerial experience in the field." A love story with a prospective promotion could start.

The first interview went quite well. I was of course very tense, in spite of knowing the subject matter well and having spent several weeks and at least five coaching sessions with a very experienced executive coach to prepare my replies to all sorts of imaginable questions. I had also followed the coach's suggestions about attitude (I had arrived wrapped in a stylish silvery coat, in my mind a clear sign of my positioning as a future senior manager) and mindset. My mother, as always in the face of critical priorities, had been accompanying my endeavor with daily prayers from Sicily. So, I felt very supported and credible as a candidate.

Apparently, the attitude, preparation, and possibly the prayers convinced the selection panel, and I was admitted to the following step. I had to endure an entire day at an external assessment center, where I was tested on vision, strategy, drafting, logic, and competitive edge. Needless to say, I hated the very idea of it. My thoughts may not have been very clear at that time, but my feelings were. I slept very poorly the night before, managed to miss the entrance to the garage, had to drive around the building, parked in an underground spot that looked spooky, and finally arrived—late—at the center's door, sweating like hell.

The rest of the day flew past like a lightning flash, eaten up by different types of interviews, essays, role-plays, and cross-examinations. I did my best. However, I did not have a sense of how successful I had been. Yet, this was paradise to me compared with what was to follow: the interview with the much-feared committee for senior appointments in an atmosphere which was far from a friendly chat. Just to give you an idea, the Chair, who was known for always probing the "killer instinct" in the candidates, reacted with a resounding "too good to be true!" to my last reply. Not very encouraging, to say the least.

This did not prevent the distinguished committee from giving me its green light. It felt like I was entering the final round of the ambition Hunger Games—by then, only myself and another candidate were still in the running for the job. The last hurdle was a meeting with the Commissioner overseeing the department. I really liked her. I found her warm, interested, and welcoming. Among other things, she noted that I had all the qualities required to be a senior manager. I left her office very hopeful that I would be the chosen one.

Only one step remained: the official decision, to be taken by the College of Commissioners. The anticipation that I would be announcing my departure due to a big promotion at the exact moment I was expected to move to a unit I had never thought of joining sent shivers of pleasure along my spine.

Weeks of radio silence followed.

The day before my 25th wedding anniversary, I received a phone call from Lara. It was late afternoon and already quite dark. I was still in my office, fiddling around with emails and some last documents to sign off, when the phone rang. It was a white office phone with an extra tab to note the most used numbers, reserved to managers—you can only picture it if you were born before 1975, I am afraid. That particular model came with an electronic display, where the number and the name of the person who was calling would show up, same as in a smartphone. My heart jumped to my throat when I read Lara's name.

"Here we go," I said to myself. "At last, I will know what's happening."

I had been left to my inner see-saw of hopes and worries since I had met with the Commissioner. I knew from experience that good news generally flies, while bad news drags its feet before knocking on your door. However, I had been trying to keep up my hopes, and informal rumors seemed encouraging.

As soon as I heard some hesitation in Lara's voice, I felt a fit in my stomach.

"Hi, Pinuccia, sorry to bother you so late."

(You never bother someone when you are bringing good news)

"No problem at all, Lara," I heard myself reply in a shy, yet encouraging tone.

A sigh followed.

(You never sigh before uttering something positive)

"Unfortunately, it didn't pan out for you."

Another pause with a long exhalation. I felt stupid as I tried to cheer her up.

"Well, I knew the selection procedure was not over yet."

How could I be so damn understanding when she was destroying my biggest career dream?

And there, Lara's voice almost broke.

"I am so sorry. You were so good, the way you showed up, your replies, your communication skills... Please do not change anything for the next time."

Another uneasy pause. This time, I did not know what more to say to soothe her embarrassment. I was feeling the blow of this overtly positive feedback. Then, what the heck? Why could I not be appointed?

She must have felt the intensity of my mental waves, because she hurried to add, "Well, actually I can give you some advice. You really had everything needed to become a senior manager, apart from experience in managing money."

I tried to object, "Well, actually I do have some budget in my current role and have a very long experience in managing projects and programs."

"Indeed, but I mean significant money. You have never managed big budgets, and that comes with extra responsibility."

True. That was the moment I became fully aware that it was the end. I was not going to get the post.

I felt extreme disappointment for a fraction of second, immediately followed by rage. Flaming, burning, scathing. Not against her personally, of course. I was hearing that I had come really close to being chosen. Everything was torn in my stomach, my guts were rumbling, my brain was thundering, my heart was pounding.

I was not listening anymore. She may have realized it, because soon after she wished me a Merry Christmas.

Very relieved, I said the same to her and could finally put the phone down.

The thought that the day after I would be celebrating my wedding anniversary immediately came to my rescue. No, that call would not succeed in poisoning a ceremony I had been designing with Serge for weeks, a moment I had been cherishing with joyful anticipation for months. To hell with the post, the selection procedure, and the non-promotion! I decided on the spot that the cruel piece of news was far less important than giving a medal to myself and my husband for having lived 25 years together in a blissful state of uninterrupted love.

Tears had no time to come to my eyes. I shut down the computer, put my coat on, and walked as usual to the metro station. I took line 1 back home as I always did, walked the nine-minute-long stretch climbing up to my house, opened the door, and jumped into Serge's arms. I must have told him something along the lines of "she called to say that I will not get the post. I could not care less because I have you." I promise, I am not copying from any Hollywood blockbuster script. As a result, he hugged me more intensely. Then he told me that everything was ready for the ceremony, celebration, and party of the following day. What more could I possibly need?

When I woke up the following morning after eight hours of good sleep, at first I felt like the day before I had produced the most spectacular "Axel-like reaction" of my life. When I think about both reactions, I realize that my behavior could seem similarly tough from outside. Just like my parents and my best friends could not believe that in a matter of days I had forgotten the boy I had been crazy about for six full months in 1989, similarly, my husband and friends could not believe I had turned the page in a matter of hours and moved on after failing to get the biggest promotion of my life.

Truth is, there was a difference between the two situations. When I was 22, I had simply shut love out of my heart because I had been deeply hurt by Axel's seeming indifference to it. I had decided to forget him as a way of punishing him, shutting him out of my life. Pride was the root of my behavior. On the contrary, what came to my rescue in the second situation was self-compassion, which always comes with deep kindness and care for ourselves. This time I was unknowingly applying the first steps of a process that I learned about at Stanford University years later: when we turn toward our suffering and are able to look at it in the eye without being overwhelmed or beating ourselves up, feeling that we are not alone in feeling the hurt, and we are able to soothe and care for ourselves like our best friend, we manifest self-compassion. And we are able to get over the pain and free ourselves much more quickly and constructively, opening the way to forgiveness.

As self-compassion involves being kind to ourselves when we suffer, the circumstances above could have reminded me (but to be honest, it did not happen at that time) of another situation involving kindness that has stayed with me for over 20 years, teasing my mind and my pride.

This was a very specific situation, which had plunged me into stress and uncertainty soon after I joined the private office of the European Commissioner responsible for Research, Philippe Busquin, a prominent Belgian politician. It was like winning the lottery to me. I had never believed I could become part of the select group of close collaborators of one of our European Ministers. Don't take me wrong: I knew I possessed the experience, knowledge, and skills for the job, but I had always thought that I did not have the right visibility for it. The fact that only nine months were left before the appointment of the new Commission, which would turn the existing private offices upside down, certainly helped.

The experience immediately enchanted me, as for the first time I was able to take part in the political decision-making level of my organization. That made me explore from the inside what I had been passionately studying at university: the different steps needed to develop a European law, the delicate balance of interests when translating the greater good into something concrete, the need for openness and cooperation at all levels. Moreover, as I was in charge of international relations in the cabinet, I could experience the thrill of representing Europe outside its borders for the first time in my professional life—and I did so in Russia, of all places!

I had been in the post for five months when it became clear that my Commissioner, who could not run for a second term for Belgium, would step down to become a member of the European Parliament. The entire cabinet was up in arms. That change meant Mayday, because the incoming Belgian Commissioner and former Minister of Foreign Affairs, Louis Michel, belonged to another party and therefore would most likely reshuffle the team inherited from Mr. Busquin, letting some of us go.

The new chief arrived with two of his closest aides. I immediately befriended one of them, Monique, a very clever and strategically-minded lady. At the beginning of September, she suggested that I accompany her on a business trip to the European Parliament in Strasbourg, France, to meet Mr. Michel for the first time.

Depending on whether he liked me or not, my first encounter with him could also be my last. I was trembling inside while wandering around the corridor maze of the European Parliament's building. Among the hundreds of doors sprinkled along extremely long corridors, Monique finally found the entrance to the office where the Commissioner was awaiting us, and knocked on the door. A powerful bass voice, which I recognized immediately, as Mr. Michel often spoke on Belgian radio and TV, ordered—more than invited—us to come in.

When we opened the door, he was having a heated discussion with the other new member of the cabinet over a meeting he did not want to go to. After the usual introductions, I mentioned the troublesome meeting, explaining that it had been in the agenda of the previous Commissioner for a long time, so accepting it was by no means the fault of my new colleague. God knows why I decided to be so candid. I was likely unaware of the risk I was taking, judging from the embarrassed looks of the other colleagues in the room. Nobody reacted, waiting for the storm. Instead, Mr. Michel looked me straight in the eye and stated, "Madam, you will go far because you are kind."

Again, somebody talking about me and going far! And this time it was not a Catholic nun praising a four-year-old child, but a seasoned politician who was famous for his volcanic temperament. Did he mean what he said? Or was he just making fun of me? And why kindness, of all things?

This question continued to bother me at regular intervals, popping up in particular when I hit the ceiling in career terms.

* * *

I went deeper into the questions of career and forgiveness at the time of my near-promotion to senior manager. That was my year of living dangerously, as you may recall that I was going through a senior management selection procedure while a far-reaching reorganization was taking place in my own department. In the end Emma, my principal, decided to move me from a unit I felt glad to lead to another one that I had never considered joining. And that, against all odds, would become the love of my lifetime in professional terms. But, as I could not then have anticipated that blissful development, I took this decision very badly, and I held a long-lasting grudge against Emma for it.

It all happened in July, while I was visiting South-East Asia with my family. Before leaving on vacation, my unfounded optimism had lured me into the illusion that I would be lucky and retain responsibility for internal coordination, an area I mastered and felt at ease with. Trying to organize a difficult restructuring by the book, Emma had embarked on a long reflection process during which she asked all her managers to indicate their other preferred units. I insisted that I did not want to move. However, as she was adamant that she had to record my preferences just in case, I talked about fundamental values. That seemed to me something I could find motivation to dive into, if worse came to worst.

However, when she interrupted my family holiday in Cambodia, insisting that she had to announce something very important to me, what followed was far worse than anything I had expected. She said that she had decided to move me to the unit dealing with product safety. I had some basic knowledge of what the unit did thanks to my internal coordination role. But I had never thought that it could be a good match for me. I was so surprised that I could just utter a very shy "why? I don't understand." She then proceeded to explain that she had noticed that my working relationships with the team of the Commissioner overseeing our department were far from ideal and, in order to protect me and my career, she wanted to put me in a place that was very interesting, but far less exposed to contacts with them. She was not wrong in saying so, as lately I had had a number of difficult conversations with my counterpart in the cabinet. I suspected that the cabinet and the Commissioner might take the side of their team member. But I would have expected the same support from my own boss!

She didn't reply to my direct question. She sounded in a hurry and quickly proceeded to explain that product safety was a very engaging and varied policy area, as it included legal work, international cooperation, project management, and very impactful initiatives. Moreover, it was easy to relate to because everybody could understand what it was about and agree it was a primary need for everybody. Her tone was dry and expeditious, making clear to me that her decision was final.

The entire conversation did not last more than five minutes. It felt like a slap in the face to me and I deeply resented her for taking that decision. I was distracted by my ongoing selection procedure and did not take a step back to consider that a reorganization always brings change along, even when you don't like it. I could have at least appreciated that, among the multiple parameters Emma had to take into account, the cabinet's preferences were a priority. Certainly stronger than my wish to stay where I was. If I had considered that, her decision would have probably hurt less.

I was also upset by the way she had communicated her decision to me. It did not help that she displayed a similar behavior soon after I had been moved to my new unit, by choosing and appointing my new Deputy over the weekend without even asking for my opinion.

Following those events, my resentment against her lasted for a few years. At the same time, my fondness for product safety and my new unit grew exponentially over the same period, and little by little my feelings for her softened. Finally, I forgave her on the very day she retired, years later.

She had invited around 500 colleagues to her farewell party, quite a bold move by someone who was notoriously introverted. Contrary to her usual frugal style, she had rented a beautiful space in a very old mansion that had been transformed into a reception building. Champagne was pouring, and the Italian delicacies she offered us were a real treat. She made a moving speech, explaining that much had changed in her life since she arrived in Brussels. She felt deeply grateful to us for having transformed her from a seasoned manager accustomed to a relatively quiet professional environment in her home country into a multi-tasking globe-trotter who had to jump from one policy to the other in the same day. She told us about her unease during the first years in Brussels. Then, little by little, her discomfort evolved into awe, respect, and friendship for her staff. We were all very moved by her words, which showed vulnerability the way Brené Brown speaks about it: rooted in humility and common humanity.

I was rushing in and out the farewell drink, moving between two important meetings. I could very easily have disappeared without saying anything to her, also considering the long queue of people that had formed in front of her. Instead, I went up to her, apologizing for skipping the queue due to my very limited time, and I said, "Dear Emma, I felt touched by your speech and I wanted to tell you that I appreciate your quest for truth."

She appeared to be moved by my inspired words and thanked me. I blushed, because those words had come out of my mouth before I could even notice. I had spoken to her a bit like Yoda. As if I were a 900-year-old sage! I ruminated on this while I was going to the following meeting, trying to capture the secret those words unveiled. And I felt that they had emerged because the sincerity of her speech had finally enabled me to see her as a human being instead of just somebody who had the power to change my professional life against my will, and I was finally able to let go of my grudge against her.

Later on, I realized that I could even wish her well. Sure, she had decided to push me away from coordination against my will. But she had the power to put me anywhere, and she could have done so carelessly. Instead, I could imagine that she had given serious thought to what I liked and what I was good at and had come up with a great match. True, she could have been more diplomatic and avoided clouding my long-haul summer vacation with her hurried call, but I was finally able to develop a generous interpretation of her behavior.

It's not by chance that I am using here the expression "generous interpretation". This expression is extensively used by Monica Worline and Jane Dutton in their book *Awakening Compassion at Work: the Quiet Power that Elevates People and Organizations*. Their research shows that, for compassion to emerge, we need to allow a generous interpretation of others' behaviors. Indeed, we hardly ever have all the information to explain why people behave the way they behave in a specific situation. If, instead of immediately going to a place of judgment, we consider that something we don't know may have influenced the situation, we open the door to compassion. And to forgiveness, which after all is a form of self-compassion.

To me, Emma was not a charismatic leader, but she has had a lasting positive impact on my life. Today I feel extremely grateful for her decision to give me a job that has fulfilled me beyond my wildest dreams and has made me grow hugely. I also recognize that forgiveness took me by surprise. I was attached to my resentment against her, and in spite of the pressure I felt, like many people of faith, to forgive those who had wronged me, I had not seen that deep feeling of release and letting go coming my way.

My experience with Emma matches what I learned during the Applied Compassion Training in April 2021: forgiveness cannot be forced on us. Possibly because it depends on the context and it involves only us, not the wrongdoer. It is a process that takes the time it takes. We can at most facilitate it by focusing on our intention to let go of resentment and to forgive. Forgiving does not mean condoning the behavior that caused the hurt, or going back to the same relationship we had with the offender before they harmed us. It truly is a gift we offer to ourselves.

As my top-notch ACT teachers, Robert Cusick and Neelama Eyres, would put it, fully enabling self-compassion is the first step toward forgiving, while failing to do so blocks the path to forgiveness, and keeps the hurt inside us. My experience taught me that refusing to lean into our suffering can reveal something else: our refusal to accept that other people may enforce their power over us. This was my case during the reorganization. The hurt caused by Emma's decision clearly lingered inside me for years, until I could finally release the anger, resentment, and grudges that were still present in me toward her for making me change jobs.

Now, people exerting power on us is a fact of life. And most of the time, we also exert power on other people, starting from the family. A skillful reaction always starts by being aware of reality as it is, without judgment—like in the metaphor of the mirror. This way we can be compassionate with ourselves, recognizing the presence of suffering, lowering its intensity by considering that we are certainly not alone in feeling excluded, rejected, and neglected, and finally being kind and understanding toward ourselves. This way we can open the door to the liberating gift that forgiveness represents for us.

The other side of the coin was less easy for me to address, when I hurt others and wished to be forgiven, like the times I shouted at my children or blurted out something mean to my husband because I had come back from the office in a state of tiredness and discontent. However, since I followed the Applied Compassion Training, I have cultivated my intention to be more mindful and aware of situations when I hurt others and, knowing that forgiveness can require a lengthy process, I now seek to redress the situation promptly, by speaking with the person I hurt as soon as I can and offering my sincere apologies.

Apologizing comes relatively easily to me, because I am generally open to others' viewpoints and I am an eager learner, as you know very well by now. But, since becoming acquainted with Fonzie, the popular character unable to pronounce the sentence "I'm sorry" who featured in *Happy Days*, the iconic teenager series spanning the '70s and '80s, I realized that for many people the possibility of not being right is a huge stressor, which results in blockages, rows, and resentment. I love the way Gloria, one of my co-workers, puts it when she observes that she doesn't care about being right, because she values good relationships much more. And she can easily let go of the need of being right and winning a theoretical battle, if this helps maintain the good vibes in the family, with friends, or at work. Because, in the end, does it matter to be right, or to have the last word? An intellectual argument can always be disputed, a belief can be countered by a different belief, a memory can be blurred, or may have left different traces in different people's brains. And letting go of the need to win at all costs actually enables us to make space for new approaches.

I remember, for example, a very painful argument between myself and a friend who was against the use of COVID-19 vaccines. I realized that, if I took a step back and put aside the fact that I had a different take on the issue, what I could sense in his angry words was the underlying fear of being cast aside. Of loneliness. So, I stopped trying to change his mind with science-based arguments and decided to tell him that I valued our relationship more than my opinion on COVID-19 and vaccines. He understood that my peaceful offer came from a place of compassion. That saved our friendship.

This does not mean that forgiving comes easily, nor that it happens in each and every case. Time plays a big role in the process, especially when the wound cuts deep in our heart. Being aware of this reality has helped me feel less guilty for not being able to forgive as much as I would wish to.

At the same time, the process of forgiving concerns me, not the relationship with the other person, because forgiveness may precede, but does not necessarily entail, reconciliation. It does require letting go and being kind to myself in a way that, in the end, liberates me from any desire to take revenge. And I can forgive and enjoy the freedom that comes with it even when the person is long gone.

By the way, as research on forgiveness advances, we are getting to understand better the evolutionary origin of forgiveness as a more skillful way to deal with conflicts than revenge. That's the reason why in the long term forgiveness always beats vengeance: it is the only sustainable way to stop the escalation of conflict. Or to mend the horrors of the past. Like, for example, in the admirable work of the Truth and Reconciliation Commission set up in South Africa in 1996 to investigate crimes committed during the apartheid era or, more recently, in Canada, to address the legacy and honor the survivors of the Canadian residential school system for Indigenous children. Forgiveness can become the engine of healing processes for entire communities.

Now that I understand forgiveness in an empowering and liberating way, I am also much more compassionate toward people who cannot forgive, and I can share what I have learned with them so that they can, if they want, at least express the wish to forgive. This openness is in the end what can ignite forgiveness, liberating us from the resentment that otherwise weighs on our shoulders, and gifting us inner peace.

My ACT teachers and many of my fellow Ambassadors of Applied Compassion have been consistently sharing how kindness and compassion have freed their hearts from resentment, and enabled them to forgive spouses, parents, siblings, friends, and beyond. Neelama Eyres has even written a book on this topic together with her former husband[7]. The beauty being that, whenever they happened to complete the forgiveness process, not only did they feel lighter and freer inside, but they were also able to inhabit again the part of their life that they did not want to look into anymore, and embrace it as a building block of who they are today.

In a nutshell, when we suffer a blow, a proud reaction is a very understandable way to protect our core, but it neither stops the hurt nor heals

---

[7] Michael Schaefer and Neelama Eyres, *Divorced with Love: Our Journey through Heartbreak and Separation into Forgiveness and Friendship*, (2017), Kindle.

it. On the contrary, forgiveness allows us to leave the burden behind us and makes space for more inner freedom.

Isn't this a great way to grow wings?

To summarize and help you practice, through meditation, journaling, or self-reflection, I have listed here the self-inquiry questions underpinning chapter 6:

- Can I recall a situation where I felt hurt and I decided not to let the hurt overwhelm me? How do I feel today when I let that experience arise again in my mind? How does my body feel?

- What does forgiveness mean to me? Can I think of a situation where (i) I forgave somebody, (ii) I asked for forgiveness, (iii) I forgave myself? How did I feel in each of those situations? Which comes more easily to me?

- To what extent does it matter to me to be right? Can I think of a situation where I let go of the need to be right? How did that feel in my body?

- Can I recall a situation where I cultivated resentment or sought revenge against someone? How does that feel in my body? Are my sensations still the same if I take a step back and reconsider the same situation?

And you can add your own self-inquiry questions below:

_____

_____

_____

_____

_____

Finally, I have selected a resource for you that I find very powerful in connection with this chapter, a beautiful forgiveness meditation practice guided by Neelama Eyres: https://youtu.be/61UMq4ToReY

For more, don't hesitate to browse through my "Recommended Resources" at the end of the book.

CHAPTER SEVEN

About Violence and Limiting Beliefs

Firework, Katy Perry

Hatred is not a feeling that I experience often. Truth is, I started recognizing this feeling because of Milan. Yes, the Italian city. Milan scarred my soul when I was just a child. And I paid Milan back by hating the city for decades.

My rational mind would easily concede that it made no sense to condemn an entire city exclusively on the basis of the bullying that I suffered in Milan in 1975, when I was eight. After all, this is not such an uncommon experience. But it is a traumatic one for sure. I had become the victim of a group of three boys, all one year older than me, who covertly insulted and hurt me every day in the school bus because I came from Southern Italy. And I'm pretty sure that being the best pupil of the school added insult to injury for them.

I had never been used to reacting openly to aggression. A good girl like me was not supposed to punch or hit other children. Even if I had dared, what chances did I have of scaring off three older boys? So, the most dignified reaction I could extract from my little scared heart all along that dreadful school year was to behave as if nothing was happening. This presented the obvious advantage that I would not bother anyone, starting with my parents.

The protracted bullying I was enduring was one of the reasons why I was so thrilled by the news that my family planned to move back to Sicily in 1976. That would definitely solve the problem. And it did, but only on the surface. Without knowing it, I had resorted to the "freeze" response among the three possible human reactions to a serious threat: fight, flee, or freeze. These are the three basic reactions in the face of a danger to life that have enabled the human species to survive the Earth's original hostile environment—and I paid dearly for repeatedly choosing "freeze" up to 2020.

For example, for years I tried to avoid conflict—a big downside for anybody, let alone a manager. It was not for lack of training or good will. But whenever I got the remark, in one or other of the unforgiving screenings held in assessment centers, that I was afraid of conflict, I would immediately whine that it was not true, because I honestly tried to address conflicts. The results, however, were meager at best, as I usually wrapped any negative feedback to colleagues in so many layers of politeness and caution that they would come out of the meeting being convinced they were the best professionals in the world.

Did my difficulty in addressing conflict offer an easy hook to get caught by a harasser? Maybe yes, maybe no. To help you form your opinion on this, let me recount the most excruciating period I experienced at work in the form of a tale.

Let's say that a new CEO, Peter, has just been appointed by the Board of your multinational company. You are very excited because you are an optimist by nature and you hope that new leadership may bring a more ambitious vision and some innovation into your workplace. You are managing one of the key project teams of the company. You brim with anticipation when you arrive, together with a few of your colleagues, at your first meeting with Peter. You start explaining the project you have been working on for one full year. You are passionate and enthusiastic. You are pretty sure that Peter will immediately see the strategic value of your project. You also present its upcoming milestone, a high-profile international conference that his prestigious role requires him to open. Peter interrupts you and accuses you of "attempting to put him in a difficult position". This rebuke is made in front of several colleagues and finds you totally unprepared. You have never stumbled upon a CEO afraid of speaking in public until that moment—and, possibly, never since. That day, you painfully learn that such a thing can actually exist. And several unexpected other traits of the new CEO start to appear day after day, characterizing him as a very peculiar boss, and leaving you every day in more pain and doubt.

Soon you realize that Peter experiences panic attacks every time he has to make a public intervention, requiring lengthy and patient pep talks from you and your colleagues to calm him down and convince him to enter the room and read his speech. He also displays a very low level of self-awareness, coupled with extreme stubbornness. For example, his knowledge of the English language is only basic. Yet, he insists on using wrong expressions in spite of the repeated attempts to respectfully correct him made by your company's well-intentioned communication experts. However, he also possesses a rare capacity to identify the best assets available to him to preserve his image and reputation, including colleagues, whom he brings directly under his power. Incidentally, this is what happens to you.

Your former boss, Bill, whom you hold in high esteem, tells you in confidence that one of the most brilliant and outspoken members of the Board had replied "over my dead body!" to those who were putting pressure on him to vote for Peter as CEO. And at some point later on, when Peter dismantles your team to oblige you to work directly for him, Bill presses you to find a job elsewhere before things go awry.

Like a modern Cassandra, unfortunately, Bill and his wisdom cannot counterbalance your naive and over-optimistic approach. You reckon that surely Peter can't be as bad as he seems, and sooner or later he will learn to feel at ease in his role. Your natural optimism regularly chokes over his deft ability to make you feel unworthy. Like when he sends your reports back several times in a row, each time giving you contradictory instructions and asking you to redraft them completely. He also visibly enjoys humiliating you in front of your co-workers. For example, he repeatedly says that he can't understand how on earth several key projects were entrusted to you in the course of your career in the company because, in his opinion, you don't even know how to write a decent report.

He often refuses to authorize your participation in important events abroad that require your presence, because "he needs you at headquarters". On the other hand, he obliges you to accompany him on fastidious business trips that have nothing to do with your tasks so that you can prep him for hours and make him shine in public. He knows that you will never say no: your loyalty to the company is undisputed and your professionalism is unflinching.

The fact that he has both power and authority over you makes your inner critic, the little voice in your mind that is always ready to highlight your mistakes, only more aggressive and unforgiving. Here is a sample of your internal chatter these days:

"I should have known better."

"I should have reacted earlier."

"I should have found the right remedy."

"How can I be so hopelessly stupid?"

"How can I still think I have any worth?"

"Where has my successful self disappeared to?"

"I am so weak and frightened that I do not deserve any consideration, not even pity."

And so on.

You start having sleep troubles for the first time in your life. Your back pain, which has intermittently bothered you for years, becomes permanent. Worse than that: your joy fades away. You smile less and less often. Your days look gloomier and gloomier, and life starts to feel tasteless, colorless, flavorless. Peter has managed to make you feel miserable and unhappy, in spite of all the blessings you are grateful for in your life.

After an extremely difficult year, you make a first attempt to put a safety barrier between Peter and you by asking for the only three months of unpaid leave you have ever allowed yourself to take in your entire career. A desperate, yet cunning move, since you know he is a real master in protecting himself from any possible official complaint. He chooses not to oppose your request and sucks his discontentment up. He is right: at work, you would never let anyone understand how deeply you are affected by his behavior in order to keep up your public person, faking strength you do not possess. And you will never dare to take a formal harassment case against him. You are afraid that such a bold move could play against your career prospects. You do not want to seek therapeutic help either, as that decision would unequivocally confirm that you are in trouble.

Basically, because of your usual optimism, pride, and wish to preserve your professional image, you choose to remain in what feels like hell to you. No wonder if, following your unpaid leave, you fall back under Peter's absolute power—and the humiliations, rebukes, and criticism that he never stops inflicting at you.

Finally you manage to swallow your pride, show yourself some compassion, and agree to listen to those who are trying to keep you from falling into the abyss.

It happens a few months after the end of your unpaid leave. You come back home from work totally squashed by another of Peter's egotistic crises. You know you cannot put up with even one more day like that. Yet, it takes your partner's deep love to finally convince you to urgently see a doctor. You manage to book an appointment with a psychiatrist who has been recommended to you. He is a seasoned professional and grasps what's happening just by looking at your face. He nonetheless patiently listens to the whole story and immediately prescribes you one month of medical leave. Then a second, then a third. And drugs to prevent you from sliding into depression.

You would have never imagined you could experience so much stress, anxiety, and fear in your life. Yet, the period of rest at home, the medication, and the caring presence of your loved ones offset the consequences of the harassment over time. At last, you can clearly see what you need to do, and you decide to move out of the company as a matter of absolute priority.

This happened to me. All of it. Maybe some of you have experienced it too: I know that harassment can occur in any organization. In case you have gone through such an ordeal, I wish from the bottom of my heart that you may heal promptly and completely.

Today I consider myself lucky for having had to face "only" moral harassment and for having survived through two endless years of agonizing hardship. It is only because I have been practicing self-compassion that I have finally stopped feeling guilty for behaving in a way similar to the time I was bullied by the three boys in my third grade in Milan. For being unable, after all those years, to respond any differently to my harasser's behavior and to protect myself. I was keeping up a brave face without realizing a truth that I learned years later in my compassion program: real courage requires embracing our vulnerability. We are all imperfect as human beings, so there is no point in trying to deny it. Accepting our imperfection and vulnerability and taking action to decrease our suffering is not weakness, it is the opposite.

I will be eternally grateful to all those who supported me along that exhausting process. I know that my own limiting beliefs would have otherwise kept me in hell for much longer. Let me flag my "common humanity joker" here, to make up for my imperfections and vulnerability: still today, years after I was harassed at work, I would not be honest if I stated that I have completely forgiven my harasser. Sure, I have made some progress and I do not fear him anymore. I can politely say "hello" to him without feeling unsettled. I cognitively understand that he must have lived through very difficult experiences to end up behaving the way he behaved toward me. Hurt people hurt people, as I have learned in my compassion studies. I have also come to a point, in the forgiveness process, where I do not resent him anymore for all the harm he caused to me. But forgiving him completely, which would entail being able to wish him well, is still in the making, and I cannot honestly predict if and when I will get there.

Escaping from my harasser was not the end of the story. Just like during my childhood, I had not really processed what had happened in a way that could enable me to respond to violence in a more skillful way than freezing on the spot—and finally fleeing. I was stuck in my self-limiting belief that there was nothing I could do other than freeze or run away when confronted with violence.

※ ※ ※

Then came 2020, the year of COVID-19 with its lockdowns and curfews. From mid-March we were all secluded in our houses and exposed to many different versions of suffering. You may remember that, after my terrible back pain crisis in 2020, I got to benefit from Helen's coaching. We embarked on an amazing journey. I guess she felt empowered to do so by the reply to the first question she asked me, "So, dear Pinuccia, what shall we focus on?"

After some silent reflection, I replied with what emerged from my heart.

"On openness."

I trusted her so much, due to all the beautiful compassion teachings she had shared with my team and myself six months earlier, that I decided to risk that unexpected reply even if I was not sure of what it really meant.

Little by little, thanks to the self-inquiry questions she asked me, the grounding meditations she led for me, the regular journaling she recommended, and the resources she helped me tap into, openness started to flow inside me and to dismantle many, if not all, of my limiting beliefs. The key question then was: what if what I believed true was not the only answer?

Thanks to my befriending of openness, the lasting cure to my harrowing issue with violence came a few months later, when I accepted to undergo hypnosis to deal with the mental scars that had been inflicted on me, from the bullying in primary school up to the moral harassment I experienced at work.

I must confess I had always been very skeptical vis-à-vis of hypnosis and similar therapeutic tools. I could not believe that this practice, that I mistakenly compared to mind-reading, could really make a difference in the life of anyone, let alone my own. However, as I was opening up more and more to practices I had never tried out before, I decided to consult a psychiatrist who specialized in these techniques. That doctor was quite senior, very competent, and deeply humane. He explained to me that hypnosis could be very useful in healing trauma, and that it generally required only one to two sessions to produce a lasting impact. He also detailed very clearly the different steps that he would guide me through and mentioned the possibility of using other techniques in case hypnosis would not work for me. The scientific explanations he offered managed to unlock my initial resistance, and I accepted to undergo hypnosis.

When the doctor asked me to close my eyes, it felt like the start of a meditation. I focused on the breath and turned my attention inward. I felt calm and relaxed, as I trusted I was in good hands. He explained that he would lead me through a visualization and, after counting to ten, he described the place he wanted me to depict in my mind: facing a closed door, that I pictured in white, with a silver-colored round metal knob. Following his indications, I put my hand on the knob and opened it. Further back I could see a flight of stairs leading upstairs. I took the stairs to the upper floor. I found a second door in front of me, similar to the one below. I opened it and entered a living room. A dark brown leather sofa that looked comfy and cozy was the first thing that met my eyes. A low, rectangular glass table stood in front of it, and a 70-inch TV screen hung on the white wall opposite to the sofa.

The doctor invited me to sit comfortably on the sofa, and announced that I would find a remote control on the low table; he asked me to hit on the power button and start watching the screen. He also explained what would appear on it: the movie about the harassment I had experienced when I was in my third grade in Milan. I immediately felt a cold grip on my heart. I did not have to describe aloud what I would see, I had only to concentrate on all the details of the film.

A film I did not know about existed somewhere inside me and unfolded on the screen in front of me. I could easily follow the sequences showing my point of view as a little girl during first and second grade and my joyful days in class before the violence. I could see and recognize my beloved teacher, a lady named Zelia, praising me for my creativity and enthusiasm to learn. One of the first scenes depicted her calling on me for a big responsibility: mentoring Giovanni. Giovanni was a sweet boy two years older than me. He had been enrolled in my class in line with the pioneering integration principles of the Italian educational system, according to which everybody would find their place in a State school, irrespective of cognitive abilities or physical aptitudes. I could see myself taking him by the hand, and later explaining some basic grammar rules to him. A close-up on his face showed all his teeth emerging from a wide smile, and his adoring look at me, as I was always extremely kind and patient with him. While watching these scenes, tears started flowing down my cheeks. The doctor silently observed all my reactions and made sure I kept focusing on the film.

Then the movie suddenly shifted to my third grade year, still in subjective camera shooting. The atmosphere in my classroom was still full of energy and gentleness, my teacher was opening up the world of geography and history to us, and I continued to excel, becoming known as the best pupil of the school. I realized we had already moved to a new school building, a square, modern construction where the gym open area was at the center and the classrooms were distributed around it, to embody the importance of exchanges and connection. But for me that was the start of a nightmare.

Next scene: I can see three young boys approaching the school bus, a light blue Volkswagen minivan from the '70s. Close-up of Marco, the leader, who looks like an angel: very cute, blond-haired, blue-eyed. Then the image gets blurred, like when it rains on the camera. Through the camera's weeping eye, I can guess that the minivan is stopping in front of the lovely, detached yellow house where I spent five years of my life, aged four to nine. Even Laika, the owner's friendly dog, is moving toward me, or at least this is what the blurred tracking shot suggests, while sweeping along the stream that divides the house garden from the street, with its tall and beautiful reeds. Then comes a close-up of an emerald green dragonfly, and the screen turns black.

A new day begins on screen: I continue watching the film shot through my eight-year-old girl's eyes. A look at the clock on the kitchen wall, it's almost 8:00! Quick, get out of the house and run to the school bus. The scene first shows—from below—my shoes stamping the gravel, then the wooden gate that is always open, and finally I jump into the minivan. I say "good morning" to the driver, who smiles back to me, and I move toward the back, where I find a place. I see the farms and the corn fields passing by the window, then I see the sky, full of clouds. The atmosphere is serene, when I get off the bus birds are tweeting and other pupils say hello to me.

The following scene starts at the end of that same school day. I get on the bus, same blue minivan as before, and I realize that the only empty seats left are in the rear. I take a seat. Just behind me, Marco and his two buddies from fourth grade shove me. They start spitting at me, pulling hard on my hair, kicking at my legs. I try to protect my face and start weeping and sobbing, while the three boys yell at me, "Go back to Africa where you belong, *terrona*[8]! What are you doing in Milan? This is not your home!"

Nobody seems to notice.

I was sobbing, sitting in the armchair with my eyes closed in front of the psychiatrist, while my hypnotized self was watching a film in which I was eight years old and being prey to the torture of bullies once again. I could feel everything that I as a little girl had felt 45 years earlier: the kicks, the hurt, the humiliation. I could not stop crying.

But the film was continuing on the screen: as a little girl, I finally got out of the minivan in front of the lovely yellow cottage, and tidied up my hair, my face, my clothes. I remembered too well that the first time this had happened, I had run toward my mother and told her everything. My mother, surely inspired by the severe education she had received as a child, had replied dryly, "Don't bring problems like this back home. You have to learn how to solve them yourself."

Those words, that I learned much later she had promptly forgotten, stayed as an open wound in my heart for all those years and had the power to wall my suffering in. It took me decades to understand that the reason

---

[8] *Terrone/a* is a word literally meaning "dark-skinned land eater", an insult used in Northern Italy against people born in Southern Italy.

why my mother replied to me in such a stern way was not lack of love for me, but simply the fact that her parents had told the same to her in similar situations. She had come to adopt the limiting belief that this was the only possible way to face issues of violence, discrimination, and injustice. Such a human reaction! Who has never experienced it, one way or another?

Then something weird happened on the screen in my mind, as if that scene had started again, like in *Groundhog Day*—was I messing up with the remote control? It appeared to be the afternoon again, I was getting on the bus and saying hello to the driver. I sat in the back and my three taskmasters surrounded me, ready to hit me, insult me, hurt me.

For a second, the scene freezes.

Then the camera closes in on Marco's eyes. Deep blue eyes, like a mountain lake on a cloudless day. Now the camera focuses on my eyes, which are a velvety shade of brown, deep like a well in the countryside. The brown, innocent and pristine eyes look into the pair of blue eyes. Now the film on the screen is showing how the blue-eyed look turns from surprised into astonished, then petrified. The camera follows it, as it moves to look at my hands. My hands are black now. And so are my arms, my legs, my face. Every part of me is black. I am black. And my hair is long and frizzy, as if I were of African descent. My eyes now sparkle with strength, joy, energy. Even my clothes glow with color: I am dressed in a turquoise T-shirt and pink shorts.

Pinuccia-me watching the screen in the visualization room is discovering a little black Pinuccia in a triumph of colors as she hops off the bus, which now is yellow, like the US school buses. And then the little, black Pinuccia girl gets closer to the camera, with a wide smile across her face.

She is so beautiful! I am weeping like a fountain, but my tears come from a place of joy now: you are black for everybody to see, while those poor boys thought they were insulting you when yelling "go back to Africa!" You send me a kiss on the tip of your fingers—finally, I am realizing that you can see me across the screen!—and you walk straight and tall out of the frame.

Little by little, my tears receded and finally dried up. The doctor asked me whether I had come to the end of the story, and when I quietly nodded, he gently called me back from my hypnotic room, counting backward from 10 to 1. On 1, I was fully back into the armchair of his office.

I still could not believe what had just happened. However, I could fully grasp its meaning. And it was liberating.

The doctor patiently waited for me to be ready to speak, as the hypnosis session had taken its emotional toll on me. Then he gently started to ask very factual questions, like "what did you see? Can you describe the scene as vividly as possible, with colors, sounds, etc.? How did you feel?"

I realized I could reply very precisely and tell him the story of the movie with lots of details, up to the marvelous, surprising end scene. When he asked, "What does this final scene tell you?" I replied without skipping a beat, "They thought they had a right to hurt me because I was different. To stop them, and all those who have hurt me ever since, I needed to show up as the real me. And it is true, I am different, including from who I thought I was. This is who I am. What is a flaw to them is the beauty of my true essence to me."

The doctor smiled, nodded, and stopped asking questions. He concluded that he was pretty confident I did not need any further session, because I had been able to dive very deep inside. He believed that I had touched the core of my issue, and that from now on I would look at violence from a different angle: not as a victim, but as a unique human being who knows herself better and can accept who she is fully.

When I stepped out of the doctor's office, I felt lighter than ever. I was smiling, feeling both relieved and immensely joyful. I could literally see the world with a new pair of eyes. I thought about what Maya Angelou wrote: "We cannot change the past, but we can change our attitude toward it. Uproot guilt and plant forgiveness. Tear out arrogance and seed humility. Exchange love for hate—thereby making the present comfortable and the future promising".

※ ※ ※

Since then, whenever memories of violence emerge from inside, I feel safe, grounded, and finally able to look at my pain without shying away. I feel able to lean into my suffering and see it as it really was, not as hurt had magnified it. I can appreciate my inner growth, and I get to experience feelings of liberation and empowerment.

I have also become better at dealing with violence. Ordinary, daily, "normal" violence. Luckily I have never found myself in a situation of extreme and pervasive violence, and I truly hope I never will. But being confronted with a dismissive gesture, an impolite answer, or a despising comment does not stop me in my tracks as it used to do. Of course, these are not pleasant experiences, but I am able to take a step back immediately and see that such behaviors have much more to do with the people displaying them than with me. This opens up the possibility for me to respond from a place of wisdom, instead of reacting like a frightened kid, as I used to do before.

What about you? What kind of reaction can you observe inside yourself when you find yourself on the receiving end of violence?

In my case, now that I was finally able to approach pain and suffering like a mirror would do, without judgment, I thought that maybe I could do more to help people around me, because I would not be overwhelmed by their suffering either. Indeed, later on, during the sessions that I offered to colleagues on compassion, many described their sense of being overwhelmed when watching or reading about catastrophes like climate change or the war against Ukraine. This is a manifestation of what is called "empathic distress" in academic terms, as explained in the Applied Compassion Training. Based on what I had learned, I suggested that they concentrate on the positive acts they had the power to carry out, rather than focusing on the feeling of powerlessness they were experiencing in the face of situations on which they could have very little impact, if any. Several reported feeling much better after deciding to volunteer at local charities, or simply calling and offering help to suffering friends or isolated colleagues. They could experience directly the difference between empathy, which stops at the level of feeling as if we were in the shoes of the suffering person, and compassion, which goes further than empathy through a decision to act. This has a liberating power that empathy stops short of.

I realize here that I have not told you in detail what brought me to enroll in the Applied Compassion Training. As you know, in 2020, after my back pain crisis, I dove deep into my heart under Helen's guidance. Her sessions went far and sometimes hurt, but in the end they cracked my heart open. Among other things, I became more and more aware of the meaning of the Golden Rule: to treat others as one would like to be treated. Without first calculating whether it is worth the effort. Without starting from the defensive position that prevents us from making the first move, as we wish to be reassured that it will not be in vain. And that first move is always a manifestation of love, kindness, and compassion.

Then, after a good number of coaching sessions that enabled me to overcome my ordeals, supported me in my decision to turn grey (as you will see in chapter nine), and inspired me to turn to hypnosis to deal with my long-standing "freeze" reaction to violence, Helen eased my leap into the arms of compassion.

She told me that at the beginning of 2020 she had enrolled in the first cohort of a degree in applied compassion offered by Stanford University. Because of COVID-19, after a first immersive weekend taking place on the gorgeous Californian campus in January 2020, the entire course had pivoted to its—unplanned—online version. At that time, I could not know that I would be following the same course in January 2021. That unexpected development required the intervention of my husband, Serge—"Coach Number One", as Helen had dubbed him.

My end-of-year reflections had led me to think that I had to found a social enterprise. However, I had not identified the goal of such an enterprise yet. In April 2020, I had volunteered as a social entrepreneurship mentor for the Santa Clara University thanks to my friend James, whom I had first met when I followed an executive leadership course at the University of Berkeley in 2017. I had grown fond of the impactful work many social entrepreneurs—committed to the greater good—carried out around the world under very difficult circumstances. When I shared this intention with my husband, after completing a self-paced online course on entrepreneurship and researching how to set up a one-person company in Belgium, he could not hide a flash in his eyes.

I knew that light. It was the harbinger of bad news, in the sense that it showed up when Serge did not share my views. Instead of going into self-defense mode, as I would usually do in these cases, I decided to really listen to what the person who loves me most had to tell me. Openness, again. And the Golden Rule: treat the others as you would like to be treated.

"You do not want to set up a charity, or any other sort of social enterprise," he said calmly.

"Why do you say this? I have been working for more than a month on it, I feel so motivated!"

"Sure, but sometimes you jump to conclusions before really looking into the question."

I paused instead of protesting. I knew he was right. My enthusiasm could sometimes lead me to skipping some necessary reflection steps.

"When I look at you, I see a wonderful person brimming with love. You want to bring more of that into the world."

"Absolutely! That's why I want to create a social enterprise!"

"Your aim is noble and generous, but this project is not what you need. In the first place, because you already have a full-time job and would not survive adding a second one on top."

"You know that I can work like crazy."

"Of course I do, I am the best placed to know that. But being an entrepreneur would be extremely challenging, even for you. You really need to devote all your time to it. Especially when you start from scratch."

I could not rebut his wisdom, so I whined, "But I know I can and should do more!"

"Who said you shouldn't? But you can choose other means."

"Which ones? I only see this path."

He smiled and paused. Then he inquired, "Have you thought about following Helen's course and becoming an Ambassador of Compassion in the Commission?"

Of course, I had told him everything about my fantastic coach, her talents, her journey with compassion.

"What do you mean? I have already done the Compassion Cultivation Training with her and the unit."

"I don't mean that course. I mean the one she is attending now."

I had never thought about that one. He had a point. I started feeling excitement mixed with fear.

"The Applied Compassion Training? But it is a one-year course, I haven't been studying seriously for 30 years!"

He laughed at my reaction.

"Come on, my beloved first-in-class student, you have always loved learning and I am sure you would rock at Stanford too. What I am seeing is that you can have a great impact in an organization you know from the inside out. Especially if you can ground what you would bring as an Ambassador of Compassion in a fully-fledged program designed and offered by Stanford University. Nobody will dare contest your credentials."

"So, seriously? You really see me as a credible Ambassador of Compassion in the European Commission?"

At that point, I was blessed with the same desperately tender look that Gregory Peck has in store for Audrey Hepburn at the end of *Roman Holiday*. I was so lucky to have Serge in my life! My heartbeat accelerated, I felt that everything was possible.

He continued, "You are a leader. You have always been, even as a child. And compassion can enable you to really decrease the suffering of your colleagues, for a start. And there are 60,000 of them. Not so bad, even for a heart as ambitious as yours. Isn't this what you really want? To do good and change the world? 'This is the way', as the Mandalorian would put it."

If you have never heard of *The Mandalorian*, Serge was referring to one of the series we had been watching on the Disney+ channel—the sentence "This is the way" has been a family private joke ever since.

So, off I went, navigating through the webpages of CCARE (the Center for Compassion and Altruism Research and Education) that explained all about the Applied Compassion Training, ACT. Every single word, image, and expression uplifted me and convinced me that Serge was right: this was the development needed by my growing crave for purpose. By my desire to spread love. By my urge to touch as many hearts as possible.

The following day, with my usual speed-of-light decision-making, I knew I wanted to enroll in ACT and be part of the amazing nascent community of Ambassadors of Compassion. I was more and more convinced that we could really change the world.

However, one last hurdle was bothering me: it looked like the 2021 course was already full. The program website only offered the possibility to be put on the priority list for ACT 2022, which would open for registration in May 2021. That was much too late for my ambition. So, on January 6, 2021 (yes, the very day of the Epiphany, which means "Manifestation", in the Christian tradition) at 4 p.m., during my usual coaching session with Helen, I explained what had happened since Christmas, meeting with her enthusiastic approval. I also depicted my frustration at not being able to enroll in the 2021 cohort. She smiled mischievously and said that she would immediately text Robert Cusick, her mentor and one of the co-founders of the program, explaining why I would be a great addition to the 2021 student list. She also recommended that I be ready to react and enroll promptly as soon as I would receive the green light from the program registrar, including completion of the application file and full tuition payment. I replied that I was ready to do anything to get on board the 2021 cohort.

"I cannot tell you for sure, but maybe the stars will align, in which case there is no time to waste. Let's have faith," she concluded.

I spent the following hours praying that Helen's query would be met with a positive answer, whatever miracle that might require. Then, at 10 p.m., I received the email that welcomed me to the program, provided I immediately fulfilled all the requirements to enroll. Needless to say, I filled the application form, inquiring about my motivation, intentions, and possible Capstone project, and transferred the money, all in less than one hour. And then could not sleep until the middle of the night because of my adrenaline surge. I knew that I had just entered a new phase in my life, one that would enable me to become a better version of myself, which in turn meant I could have more positive impact on the world.

When I look back, I find it wondrous how a series of threads, sometimes dramatic, like my experience of being harassed, sometimes healing, like the impact of Helen's or my husband's wisdom on my personal growth, all converged on my decision to cultivate compassion. In the past, my pride and naïveté had prevented me from accepting my vulnerability and looking for more sustainable alternatives than freezing in the face of violence. The people who had met me where I was, with deep humanity and the sincere aim to help me, had made the difference, embodying love and compassion for my greater good. Thanks to them, my inner balance tipped toward more introspection, more courage, and ultimately enabled me to reconnect with my life purpose, surrendering to love and compassion. All of this unfolded from the walking seminar on purpose in 2019, then through the Applied Compassion Training in 2021, up to my ongoing studies and practice of compassion.

Along the way, I have witnessed the power of compassion manifesting in many people around me. I will mention here Laura Berland, a very inspiring teacher I met and befriended in the last quarter of 2023, during my certification training course in compassionate leadership. Laura was a successful broadcaster in New York for more than 20 years before getting interested in meditation. The practice of meditation brought her to deepen her knowledge of compassion. The call to compassion then led her to found, together with her husband Evan—a remarkable compassion teacher too—the Center for Compassionate Leadership[9], and teach how compassion can change our individual lives and the world. Laura has inspired me to embody compassionate leadership wherever and whenever I can, as you will see in the next chapter.

Another admirable person I am very fond of is Sarah De Carvalho[10], who led a very successful career as a producer and presenter for the BBC until she encountered the street children in the favelas of Rio de Janeiro and decided to devote her life to helping them get out of a life of misery, violence, and hopelessness by providing them with homes, care, and education. I was lucky enough to interview her several years ago for my blog on brave women, and I could connect with a person whose authenticity, generosity, and compassionate heart shines through.

And you, do you know of anyone who has fallen in love with compassion in their own way? Could this person be you? Just consider whether you could listen with openness and curiosity to somebody talking about compassionate leadership[11].

I am deeply convinced that everybody has boundless value as a human being, and a life purpose that makes them a unique gift to humankind. Learning from hard experiences with the help, love, and support of people who treat others as they would like to be treated—and

---

[9] https://www.centerforcompassionateleadership.org/.

[10] https://www.aacsb.edu/about-us/advocacy/member-spotlight/influential-leaders/2018/sarah-de-carvalho.

[11] For example Dr. Michael West here: https://www.youtube.com/watch?v=EiHdGPrV-RY.

there are so many of them, if we only open up and notice—brings to light the truth of who we are.

To summarize and help you practice, through meditation, journaling, or self-reflection, I have listed here the self-inquiry questions underpinning chapter 7:

- Can I recall a situation when I felt the emotion of hate? How did that feel in my body? As every emotion is a messenger, what is hate trying to communicate to me?

- How do I react in the face of violence? What kind of reaction can I observe inside myself when I find myself on the receiving end of violence? Can I bring to mind a specific situation where I was treated violently? Was I able to offer some self-compassion to myself?

- Have I ever said things like "I should have known better, I should have reacted earlier, how could I be so hopelessly stupid,..." to myself? In which circumstances? Could I replace that reaction with a more skillful response, such as caring and soothing?

- Have I experienced or witnessed harassment at work? If so, what action could I take to decrease my suffering or the victim's?

- Do I know of anyone who has fallen in love with compassion in their own way? If yes, what do I find inspiring in them? Could this person be me?

What It Takes to Be Yourself

And you can add your own self-inquiry questions below:

_____

_____

_____

_____

Finally, I have selected a resource for you that I find very powerful in connection with this chapter, a blog post titled "Compassion over hate" published on the Center for Compassionate Leadership (CFCL) website: https://www.centerforcompassionateleadership.org/blog/compassion-over-hate

For more, don't hesitate to browse through my "Recommended Resources" at the end of the book.

CHAPTER EIGHT

What Death Has to Do with Compassionate Leadership

The Night King, Ramin Djawadi
(from the soundtrack of "Game of Thrones")

Have you ever seen a dead person?

I have. Once. And I still remember it.

I was 22, but it feels as if I was 12. My maternal grandfather had been brought back from the hospital just in time to die at home. In those times, the unforgettable '80s (at least for me), nobody wished to die in healthcare, and families would do anything to bring even a quasi-corpse back home and give the loved one a chance to close their eyes forever in their own bed. Probably hospital paperwork and liability waiver clauses were very light or non-existent at the time. However, I suspect the wish to die at home would still be everyone's, if at all possible. It is certainly mine.

I remember the horrid fascination I felt when, sneaking among the relatives who were sitting or standing around his bed, I managed to catch a glimpse of the corpse. It did boast some resemblance to my grandfather, but it had nothing left of the usual stern expression on his face. The lying body appeared to be much smaller than when he was alive: he was 180 cm (5'11") tall, which meant he—born in 1912—was among the tallest Sicilian men of his time. But the eeriest detail was that a blue cotton ribbon had been tied around his face and somebody had knotted it high up at the front, making him look like a surreal Easter egg. Later, I learned that such a gimmick was needed to avoid his jaw loosening and leaving his mouth wide open, which, I have no doubt, would have looked even more unsettling. In any case, my last memory of my grandfather is akin to a sort of Hieronymus Bosch's painting. Maybe my personal way to get rid of the fear and unease that he had always provoked in me due to his severity and sternness?

And yet, how unfair of me! My grandfather, like most children in very poor families, was sent to work instead of school at the age of six. This meant that he could start learning how to write and read only when he retired, and both activities remained a struggle for him until the end, as these are skills best acquired in childhood.

Moreover, the traditional way of confining boys within so-called "masculine behaviors" meant that my grandfather grew up with the moral duty of being tough, even violent if required by circumstances (including to "redress" his children), and to assert his pride and honor at any cost. Being a handsome man—he was often compared to Clark Gable—it went without saying and was almost acceptable that he might fall for women, even when he was a married man. On the other hand, he was a hard worker and combined several jobs to feed his family—not only his wife and six children, but for many years also his mother, his unmarried sister, and his second, married sister together with her husband, too proud to accept the kind of humble jobs that my grandfather would not shy away from, and their four children. All in all, what I would be tempted to call a wicked life. And yet, what do I know—really—about him? Whether he would have called himself satisfied, unlucky or unworthy? The only thing I can be sure of, is that without him I would simply not exist. A part of him is forever in me. And this is the sort of mystery that becomes deeper the moment you think you have understood something of it.

The reason why I bring up my grandfather now is that it was unsettling for me to bear witness to the reality of his death. As if I did not know how to feel in front of the undeniable fact that he was not there anymore. And that death will come for each and every one of us.

It was the first time in my life that death literally invited itself into my experience, and it was challenging. I bet many of you have thought, just like me, that life would be much easier if death did not exist. Still, here we are, all of us, with this sword of Damocles hanging over our heads since the day we were born. Or, shall I say, with this reminder that we'd better focus on what really matters, considering that our life as we know it may end any time—and one day it surely will. One way or another, this is another clear pointer to our inescapable common humanity!

Of course, the fact that death is inevitable, and therefore an essential part of life, does not mean that it is easy not to fear it. Clearly, I belong to that part of humankind that fears death —possibly because I love life so passionately. For many years, this fear lingered somewhere between my mind and my heart, until one day it emerged as fear of flying. It happened in 2005 on a flight between Brussels and Crakow, Poland. I started shivering and mentally uttering my last prayers when the airplane wheels left the runway. From that flight onward, my heart jumped to my throat at the slightest shaking of a plane. Turbulence became my nightmare, and I used to squeeze the armrests for the entire duration of the landing, to the point of leaving nail marks in the seat covering. Why on earth was this happening to me, after many years of peaceful, even pleasant flying experiences? No amount of self-inquiry could help me uncover the secret causes of my sudden fear of flying. I ended by giving up on my attempts to find a reasonable explanation to this new, unwelcome feeling. And then, in October 2021, I found a remedy. Exactly, a remedy. Not a full treatment for my fear of flying, but what my compassion teachers would aptly call "a skillful response".

I was already meditating twice a day by then. This practice had become one of the most helpful resources to keep my balance. When I meditated, focusing on one thing at a time, be it my breath, my body or self-inquiry questions, I managed to calm my nervous system down and created more space inside me. This, in turn, helped me take a step back from what was happening and respond from a place of wisdom. By pure chance, one day I discovered that I could download meditations on my iPhone and listen to them even when my device was set to flight mode.

What It Takes to Be Yourself

Leaving Brussels to fly to Sicily, a trip which I was anticipating with deep joy as I had not been able to see my parents for too long due to the pandemic, I decided to try meditating as soon as the plane lifted itself from the tarmac. I closed my eyes and followed the soothing voice of the meditator, first asking me to focus on the breath, then to feel present and to surrender to whatever was happening. I did, and a miraculous sense of calm and peace filled me, leaving no space to fear and worry. That state outlasted the 20-minute meditation, and allowed me to enjoy a flight for the first time in years.

Needless to say, since that day the first thing I make sure to pack when preparing for a flight is my earbuds (no chance I would forget my iPhone). And I have not experienced any flight panic attacks ever since.

Does this mean I am not afraid of dying anymore? No, of course not. And I have good reasons for that: without being a reckless adventurer, I still remember very clearly a relatively recent situation where I escaped death by seconds. And it is not the kind of experience I look forward to.

I was enjoying a moment of rest with a colleague I was travelling with, an upbeat lady named Dorina, during the afternoon between two official meetings in Ottawa, Canada; it was June 28, 2018. I take the opportunity here to share that I have always been an eager soccer supporter. As young as six, I already knew by heart the composition of my club, Juventus, and of the *Squadra Azzurra*, as we Italians call our beloved national soccer team. I had lived with unfathomable joy through the World Cup in Spain in 1982, the year Italy won this most prestigious soccer global competition after a wait of more than 40 years. Even though living in Belgium had made it practically impossible for me to continue following the adventures of my club every Sunday, not to mention the fact that I had turned into a hyper-busy mother of three and a manager, I would do anything not to miss the most important matches of the World Cup, once every four years—especially when Italy was playing.

That evening (4 p.m. in Ottawa), Belgium were to play England. Since my husband is Belgian and I am Italian, my children have always been particularly eager supporters of both the Belgium and Italy soccer teams. Thus I thought that the blissful break in my day would give me the opportunity to be connected with them in spite of the ocean stretching between us. So, I quickly replaced my elegant dress with some more touristy clothes to survive the 35°C (95°F) Ottawa was gasping through, and charmed Dorina into having a bite at a cool place nearby our centrally placed Novotel hotel, a restaurant that I had noticed when arriving from the airport by car. The place sported several huge screens, most of which had been tuned to the World Cup soccer matches. Dorina, who was glad to have the possibility to eat something, joyfully agreed, and we entered the air-conditioned restaurant, which was stylish, very large, and practically empty on that summery, suffocating afternoon. We spotted a good table, placed at a convenient distance from one of the screens already showing the first minutes of the Belgium-England match. We ordered something vaguely exotic, and the waitress brought water with ice cubes. It looked like a blessing, even though inside the restaurant the air conditioning was set to an outrageously low temperature, and almost mechanically I started sipping water from the glass. From time to time, I sucked an ice cube up and rolled it inside my mouth to make it melt more quickly: a habit I had since I was a child and that I had never paid attention to. While avidly watching the match (Belgium were already leading 1 - 0), another ice cube lodged itself in the back of my mouth. Most likely due to my focus on the screen, I inadvertently swallowed it. But for one of those unpredictable hazards of life, it did not go down the usual path. When I started choking, unable to push any air down my throat, I understood that the damn ice cube was blocking my airways.

I lifted my hands to my chest, as if they could help. Dorina realized something was wrong, and started asking, "Are you OK? What's happening?"

But even if I tried hard, no sound could escape my throat, which had become my very own black hole. Drops of sweat appeared on my forehead, while my brain was frantically trying to find a solution. Dorina gave me powerful pats on the shoulders (she was not trained to perform the Heimlich maneuver, which is the only solution in these cases) and screamed for help, managing to attract a waitress after around 30 seconds. To me, those 30 seconds felt like 30 hours. Now, do you have an idea of how many thoughts a human being can produce in such a short time span? Research shows that we can produce around 6,000 thoughts a day. So, many can occur to us in 30 seconds. I did not count them, but they were a lot! And they were mostly as useful as "what a stupid way to die", "frankly, if you had really learned the Heimlich maneuver during the first aid course you took ten years ago you would not be in this situation", and "how come there is no bloody nurse or doctor in this place?"

Then, when I was starting to think that I was watching my own passing away, my breath came back with a loud "aaaargh!" sound. In and out, almost magically. Almost, because my airways, my throat, and the back of my mouth kept on hurting severely for at least one hour, and left my whole torso extremely sore, like a bodily echo of the near-tragedy.

I was in shock. I was sweating much more abundantly than before choking on the ice cube. Stupor entered me, like an alien occupying my body. How come I was still alive? One more minute at most and no amount of Dorina's crying, powerful as it was, could have brought me back from the other side.

My hands were now touching my throat, as if they were still unable to believe that the danger had disappeared. Dry coughing was renewing my pain every five seconds, making me dizzier and dizzier. The waitress offered to bring me more water. I stared at her in utter dread, only able to blurt out "please, no ice cubes", which in hindsight made me laugh and cough even more.

Dorina was still ranting about the lack of medically skilled customers in the restaurant and asking me if I felt better, when it dawned on me that my body heat had been my savior, as it had accelerated the melting of the ice cube. If I had choked on meat or any other solid bite, I would have died.

Dead. At only 51. When I was a child I thought that somebody turned old already at 30, and that 51 was a normal age to be a grandmother, hence not that far from death. But I can assure you that, in that moment, it really felt too soon (and today it would too, by the way). While getting used to breathing normally again, an unstoppable sequence of things I might not have been able to do, complete, or enjoy anymore went live in my brain, like a series of movie trailers, this in spite of the persistent cough and pain in my chest.

After this fateful day, I decided to take advantage of every opportunity to benefit from life and share the joy of being still alive with those around me.

Obviously, forming the firm intention of living in the present moment and enjoying every opportunity that life throws at you does not necessarily entail a miraculous change. In the following weeks, months, and years, I missed very many chances to mindfully appreciate and be grateful for even the slightest ray of sunshine or child's laughter in the street—and still do. However, these lapses were not due to lack of determination on my part. The intention to enjoy every single moment of my life has never left me since that resolution, and I dare say that I am getting better at this day after day. As a matter of fact, a couple of years ago I took part in a large international conference lasting several days in the US. After a very intense day where I had spoken at a few sessions on product safety topics, I joined a group of participants going to a dueling pianos venue. I was the first one to hit the dance floor and the last to leave it several hours later, with one of the participants telling me "you lead even when you dance!" in a tone that betrayed both surprise and admiration.

This anecdote sheds some light not only on my ability to play hard and work hard, but also on the nature of leadership, which for decades I had regarded as a sort of innate quality, a heavenly gift destined for the happy few who may change the course of history. The compliment I received then, though, linked leadership with a mundane activity like dancing. I was intrigued and felt the need to deepen my inquiry into the nature of leadership. After all, maybe leadership was not reserved for the happy few. Maybe it was possible to lead in a down-to-earth way. Curiosity and the exploration of my life experience and its lessons, including what I learned thanks to my fear of death, led me to recalibrate my idea of leadership. And this happens to reflect scientific developments in this field.

* * *

State-of-the-art research defines leadership as "the art of motivating a group of people to act toward achieving a common goal"[12]. This sounds quite reasonable, and even attainable by most of us, right? However, such a definition does not explain what makes people trust in somebody as a leader, be it only on the dance floor. So, let's explore this angle and suppose that you believe, like me, that courage belongs to the very nature of leadership. For decades I judged myself harshly when it came to courage. For starters, I have been risk-avoiding in many circumstances. Taking few or no risks does not sit well with bravery. Hence, how could I possibly consider myself courageous? Then, little by little, a very powerful path to courage emerged in front of me. Neither quickly nor easily, though. And it did not spare me fear and worry. Just to give you an example, after Brussels was struck by two terrible ISIS suicide attacks on March 22, 2016, one at the airport, the other in the subway, at the very station I used to get off at for years to reach my office, I felt the grip of fear in waves. Sometimes I took the subway without even thinking of the attacks, but oftentimes I

---

[12] "What is leadership?", https://www.thebalancemoney.com/leadership-definition-2948275.

felt my stomach complain and my forehead get colder, and I suddenly changed my route and walked to the bus stop instead. I could invoke self-preservation to justify my behavior—certainly not courage.

Quite surprisingly for me, it was the fact of being responsible for my entire team that pushed me into the arms of courage in unexpected ways. Take, for example, the first time a new big boss came to meet my unit some years ago. We only had 60 minutes to make a lasting impression on her. I proposed to my colleagues that I would introduce our mission and way of working, and then each of them would have two minutes to introduce themselves and stress one important file or area they were responsible for. This would still leave 15 minutes for questions and answers. They accepted merrily, and on the day of the encounter we followed the agreed script. Our newly appointed top manager praised our way of presenting the unit and its activities, and her genuine smile confirmed our unexpected approach had left a lasting mark on her.

When she left the room, one of my colleagues came to hug me and solemnly said in front of all team members, "Thank you very much, Pinuccia! I do not know of any other manager who would have given up the opportunity to show off in front of their new principal, and make space for her 20 colleagues to be seen and heard instead."

I realized in that very moment that I had been brave and had led by example. But I had not felt brave. I had chosen to show up with courage. And my colleague's recognition came as a huge reward for my choice. So I started to understand that leadership can coexist with fear—of flying, dying, losing people, you name it. But it does not stop there. And when it pushes us to act with courage and selflessness, it starts to look like compassionate leadership: if you remember, this means leading for compassion with compassion. Courage, however, is not the only quality required to turn us into compassionate leaders. As I learned during my Compassionate Leadership Certification Program in 2023, to lead for compassion with compassion we also need curiosity, humility, generosity, humanity, self-awareness, and active listening, just to mention its most important qualities.

So, how did this whole process pan out for me? I have already shared how I arrived at my first managerial position—mainly driven by my need to be recognized and feel appreciated. You may remember that I had another driver too, which became stronger as I felt more and more recognized in my new role. I wanted to serve my team to my best ability, not only because of what I had learned in my numerous management courses, but because I really enjoyed taking care of people. And you cannot do this if you are not compassionate. Practicing compassion increases your capacity to notice suffering in others and act to decrease that suffering. And this, in turn, makes people feel valued and safe, spurs their creativity, improves the quality of their work, and boosts their performance and resilience.

As I got better at spreading compassion and unleashing my team's talents, others started to see these qualities in me. I very vividly remember in particular a scene that happened at the Hilton Odaiba Hotel in Tokyo in December 2017. I was participating for the first time in a large international conference on product safety. I had been working for weeks with my team on the content of the keynote speech I had been invited to deliver in front of hundreds of experts, most of whom had never seen me before. I had already learned a lot on the essentials and the challenges posed by dangerous products. I knew that this was the ideal international audience for putting an issue on the table that was still heavily underestimated, if not ignored, in the product safety community: the influence of new technologies on the very concept of product safety. My experts had prepared a beautiful PowerPoint presentation with inspiring images, and speaking points that I had adapted to my style on the plane from Belgium to Japan.

The day of the keynote I put on a statement black-and-red dress and strode to the speaker lectern while my heart was racing in my chest. Fifteen minutes later, the prolonged applause that welcomed my speech confirmed that I had made an excellent first impression on my new community. And I had hopefully managed to wake up their interest in the issue I wanted to put on the table.

Then reality surpassed my expectations when Michelle, the Chair of the international organization hosting the event, came to me and solemnly stated, "You are a global leader!"

This sentence mysteriously resonated in me for years. Partly because I could not believe my ears, after the mayhem I had gone through not so long before, where my pride and my ambition had sustained two major blows, as you may remember: my non-promotion to senior manager and my move due to the reorganization of my department. Partly because I could immediately tell from Michelle's role in the organization, her acute sense of humor, and ability to address any issue during the conference, that she was a leader used to negotiating and taking strategic decisions. Which in my experience are two indispensable qualities on the international scene. Such a powerful and talented woman, who has since become a dear friend of mine and an Ambassador of Applied Compassion too, could not have spoken lightly.

The meaning of her statement became fully clear to me six years later when, to my utter surprise, the same organization awarded me its Achievement Award in Product Safety during its annual conference. That was one of the most exhilarating and moving moments in my life. A moment of true humility and profound happiness, that inspired my acceptance words. Let me share them with you here, as a token of my gratitude to God, life, and my extraordinary product safety international community.

"I am deeply touched by this award, and I want to thank the members of the Board from the bottom of my heart for giving me this amazing recognition. And for awarding me this for the reasons that last year's awardee has just mentioned in passing the baton to me: consumer health and safety, international cooperation, and compassion. You know me quite well! For this reason, I want to share with you something you probably don't know.

I have not been that long in the field of product safety, especially if I think of those of you who have worked in this area for decades. What you don't know is that I did not choose to land in product safety. My arrival was the result of a restructuring. I am sure that this is an experience many of you have had, and it is never pleasant. However, when I started back in 2017, my team, whom you know is amazing, welcomed me with open arms, and very quickly I realized that product safety has it all: it has law-making, it has science and innovation, it has international cooperation. And it is compassionate by design, because its goal is to keep consumers safe. And consumers is the way human beings are called in economics, so actually product safety has common humanity at its core. So, what happened is that I immediately fell in love with it, and instead of working from a place of duty and obligation, as is often the case after a restructuring, I delved into product safety with passion and purpose. Like all of us here.

By giving me this award, you are telling me that I have an impact, that what I do with my team makes a difference, and I thank you very much for this once again. But let me also tell you something: actually, we are getting this award together. Because nothing of what I have thought, imagined, proposed, or designed would have happened without you here, without my incredible team, my colleagues in the other Commission departments, without the businesses, consumer organizations, researchers, experts, specialized press ...

Truth is, we are all in this together. Yes, because in this wonderful community we can open up and hold each other. We can share our joy and our sorrows, our challenges and our discoveries, our failures and our victories, our questions and our insights. We can have philosophical discussions and we can drink, eat, laugh and dance together. And we can find resources.

So, as a matter of fact, you are my award. Thank you for having me in this awesome community. I have no doubt that we will continue together to make consumers safe, and to make the world a better and safer place for everyone."

A gorgeous bunch of Stargazer lilies sent to me by my dear friend and fellow Ambassador of Applied Compassion Michelle to celebrate my award (my photo)

Why was I so touched? I guess because all along the six years that followed the Tokyo event, thanks to my colleagues and all the members of the product safety professional community, I had been experiencing that working together in an area as meaningful as product safety for the greater good had a real impact and could lastingly change the world for the better. It was like a dream come true. And compassion had become part and parcel of me and the conduit of my life purpose.

I also discovered that compassionate leadership, which is nourished by common humanity, humility, and compassion, works both upwards and downwards. I wonder whether this might be one of the reasons why the different Chairs of the US agency in charge of product safety never refused to meet with me, even though my rank could not match theirs, and how we could easily connect on a purely human level.

This was certainly the reason behind a difficult decision I took in the last stretch of the political negotiations on the new law on general product safety. When we get to this point in the European Union, generally a decisive, restricted meeting takes place, often during the night, between the leaders of the Council, the European Parliament, and the Commission teams, so that the deal can be discussed and agreed in detail before sealing the final political agreement. The three leading negotiators take maximum two collaborators each with them to a small room, and the rest of the teams stay in the main meeting room, fretting about what will come out of the restricted meeting, sweating and praying.

When my boss turned to me, asking who should go with him, in just a couple of seconds the following happened to me: I felt deep gratitude for his relying on my advice; my heartbeat went crazy, as that was an experience I had never had and was longing for. It was the first and possibly the last time I could take part in such a coveted negotiation, considering that I was in the last stretch of my career and that new laws are meant to last for decades. Right then, I took a breath and a mental step back. I considered the situation and told myself that the most skillful decision would be to ask the team leader in charge of the file and the unit's legal coordinator to go with our boss. They were the finest experts on the draft law under discussion, and the best assets we could count upon. I mourned for one second my unfulfilled dream, and I asked my two colleagues to accompany him. I could see in their eyes first surprise, then joy and gratitude. They had obviously expected me to take one of the two available seats and had not anticipated my decision at all.

My heart was still aching, yet I knew deep down that I had done the right thing. And helping new leaders grow because of my decision to step aside quickly pushed my disappointment away and made me feel happy. I was aware that I had used my power wisely and for the greater good.

Yes, I do believe that leadership means power. However it can mean power in many different ways. Early in my life I had to cope with traditional authority figures like my grandfather, my father, and Father Tommaso. My desire to escape the kind of power they exerted on me, because I was a woman and because youngsters were expected to obey older people, was one of the drivers that pushed me to seek freedom outside my country. But I had never dreamt of being a powerful person *per se*. Obliging others to do what I wanted or deemed right could in no way make me feel more worthy or formidable. My special relationship with unconditional love had already catered for that. I just wanted to be free to be myself, without having to fit in a mold destined for women of modest social origin, like me.

My close encounter with death made me more than aware that every second mattered in expressing my authentic being and acting accordingly. My professional career strengthened my chances to fulfill my life purpose and produce a lasting, positive impact on people and on the world. Something that I was the only one able to manifest on Earth and in human history, because each of us is a unique gift to humankind.

Having reached a position of power in my organization, I knew that I was free to embody a quality of leadership that reflected who I am. And in recent years I have befriended, studied and even taught compassionate leadership: leading with compassion for compassion.

I have also come to understand that everybody may be a leader, in ways and areas that belong to them. For example, I have always been filled with admiration for one of my former house helpers, an adorable, clever, and spirited lady called Karla. She worked for over a decade for us, to my and Serge's complete satisfaction and to the delight of our children, whom she loved deeply and regularly showered with presents. Karla excelled in her job and was always fun and joyful. But she was also determined to pursue her dream to complete university studies in business and find a different type of job. So, after years of hard work and study, she completed her degree and almost immediately found a job as a bar manager right in the heart of Brussels. She quickly became responsible for the management of a chain of very well-known bars specializing in Belgian beers, and she has been happy and fulfilled ever since. No doubt her new responsibilities are more in line with her life purpose and entail genuine leadership. I feel proud for having encouraged her to pursue her dream from the beginning, even though I was perfectly aware I would lose her as an outstanding house helper. By the way, her departure has had an amazing win-win development, as I have found another first-class house helper who feels happy and appreciated for doing her job, and finds purpose in it.

That's the reason why I have come to cherish immensely the power of agency that compassionate leadership lends me, not to increase my fame, wealth, social status, or power over other people, but to inspire and support them to be their best self and align with their life purpose.

And you, can you see in which areas you lead, or may develop your leadership skills? And what motivates you deeply? What fulfills an essential need of yours or allows you to be generous, to help, to care for others? I'm ready to bet that through self-inquiry you will find that spot, which is intimately connected with your purpose. Try and let me know!

To summarize and help you practice, through meditation, journaling, or self-reflection, I have listed here the self-inquiry questions underpinning chapter 8:

- Have I ever seen a dead person? How did I feel? What did that experience bring to me?

- Am I afraid of dying, for example when I fly or drive? Where does that come from? What can it teach me? Can I devise and try a strategy to reduce my fear of dying?

- Have I ever been on the brink of death? What did I feel then? What consequences did that have on my behavior, beliefs, intentions?

- What are the qualities of a real leader in my opinion? Do I see those qualities in myself? Does somebody else see those qualities in me? In which circumstances?

- Can I see in which areas I lead, or may develop my leadership skills? And what motivates me deeply? What fulfills an essential need of mine or allows me to be generous, to help, to care for others?

And you can add your own self-inquiry questions below:

_____

_____

_____

_____

Finally, I have selected a resource for you that I find very powerful in connection with this chapter, an article titled "Rising Above Fear And Leading With Courage And Confidence" by Kiran Mann in Forbes:

https://www.forbes.com/councils/forbescoachescouncil/2023/07/31/rising-above-fear-and-leading-with-courage-and-confidence/

For more, don't hesitate to browse through my "Recommended Resources" at the end of the book.

PART III

Surrendering to Life Purpose—and Thriving

The two most important days in your life are the day you are born and the day you find out why.

—Attributed to Mark Twain

A double rainbow in the sky over Brussels, June 2020 (Serge's photo)

CHAPTER NINE

Dropping the Magic Mirror to Face Shame

Video, India. Arie

Dyeing my hair was not something I was ever thrilled to do. I had tried hard to resist the appeal of touching up the color when I discovered the very first white hair on my head. I was only 35 then, and some colleagues, rumor had it, nicknamed me "the gorgeous Contino". For me it was out of the question to give up on such a flattering reputation just because of some stupid white hair. So I started, first with coloring shampoo, then temporary dye and, finally, when I was around 40, I went full dye.

    I often fumed in my head against the dyeing slavery that women (and apparently more and more men) are subjected to. At the same time, whenever I thought about bravely escaping the coloring camp, images of puffy babushkas or withering grandmas would materialize in front of me—the living denial of attractiveness! So, courage went out the window and I continued going regularly through the dyeing routine. Which is not the worst torment in the world, of course; but apart from the pricey hairdressing services and the time that it requires, the experience in itself is not very pleasant, considering that you have to bear for half an hour with a sticky and smelly mixture on your head. It is uncomfortable at least and, sometimes, because of the strong chemicals used in most products, my scalp could itch or I could feel dizzy from their intense smell. But what extra mile wouldn't a woman go in order to be more beautiful? I can assure you that at times I was mad at myself when I realized that my feminism did not go as far as accepting my natural color of hair once it started to turn white.

Yet, the day came when I finally surrendered to my whitening hair. What made the trick, quite unexpectedly, was the discovery that someone I loved deeply had developed a very serious health issue. My own wish to decrease that person's suffering pushed me on August 13, 2020, to make the vow to dye my hair no more. Six months before starting my journey into the science of compassion through Stanford's Applied Compassion Training, I actually took an important decision out of compassion. A decision that would have lasting repercussions on my life.

What I learned in January 2021 at Stanford was that compassion means noticing suffering in others or in yourself, and deciding to do something to decrease that suffering. And that, when we cannot have an immediate and direct impact on that suffering, the simple fact of having the intention to help is a compassionate reaction. This was the case here, and is often the case for example when we learn about catastrophes happening in other parts of the world. So, sending good vibes or wishes for the healing of someone qualifies as an act of compassion. In my specific situation, I wanted to emphasize my support through a personal choice, which was totally altruistic because I would not have taken that difficult step for myself. I was hoping that in some mysterious way—that I did not even need to know—my sacrifice would transmit something positive and contribute to the healing of the person suffering, so that a dramatic health situation would not develop further into tragedy.

I will never be able to prove that my vow had any influence on the situation from which it stemmed. The fact is that, after some time, the health of my loved one improved. I am content with this result, which has reinforced my faith in the impact of altruistic wishes, whatever they are called: vibes, waves, prayers, vows, offerings, or sacrifices, whether in a religious context or not. However, the next part of the path was to prove less than smooth for me: the day following that (for me) historic decision, I spent more time regretting it than congratulating myself on my brave heart. Sadly, once the euphoria and pride produced by my compassionate decision faded away, I started realizing its horrifying consequences.

Here I need to tell you something that you might consider totally frivolous: I could not picture myself, rather, my public image, gaining ten years in six months. Truth is, as a child and mainly because of my family's opinion on my looks, I used to bask in the conviction that I was a rare beauty—a clear overstatement. Obviously, nobody among my classmates seemed to agree with this assessment when I started secondary school. I ended up living through very miserable teen years that made me doubt, sometimes even despise, every part of my face and body. Nothing stood particularly out in my physical appearance, apart from my spectacled look, which was the last thing a teenager would call an asset. I was plagued with very bad eyesight requiring thick glasses until I was 14 years old—after that, luckily, contact lenses came to my rescue and improved my perception both of reality and of my physical appearance. My eyes could maybe show depth and boast an attractive shape now that they were not hiding behind thick glasses, but they were desperately brown, just like those of the majority of human beings: nothing special, and certainly no fair color, the favorite among Italians being blue. My hair was also hopelessly brown—no possible connection there to sexy icons like Marilyn Monroe or Madonna. And my curls were so wild that early in my life my mother decided that the best way to keep them under control was to have them cut very short every month. My transforming teenage body inherited curves and softness from hundreds of generations of Mediterranean women before me—certainly not in line with the sporty and slim female shapes that triumphed on TV, in the press and every advertisement. And I disliked sport. So I had no hope of improving the situation.

When my body finally came of age, I did not realize it was an acceptable deal, to say the least. I was suspiciously watchful over every kilo, ever aware that I loved cakes and ice cream almost as much as I hated sports. So, the only area I could possibly excel in terms of image was elegance, which is considered to be a desirable component of beauty, a non-negotiable value worshipped like an absolute truth by every Italian woman—to my knowledge. With all the sacred principles, strict rules, and rigid enforcement that go with it.

When I embarked on my professional career in Belgium in 1991, I must admit that I started having my fair share of compliments and admirers. In those days I could still walk on high heels, wear a size 6 and boast a mane of shining, dark curls. For sure, I was also convinced that professional success required high standards in relation to image, body, weight, and beauty. I was totally unable to see how this view of things was the product of my culture way more than a universal benchmark. And only in the last couple of years have I understood how much such a vision is discriminatory and unfair. In particular when, as a cultural habit, I would immediately scan any woman on the horizon to rate her based on my aesthetic standards, and feel a fit of satisfaction if I found myself ahead in the race, or skip a heartbeat if I had to acknowledge to myself that she was more attractive, slim, or elegant than me.

However, arriving in Belgium also initiated a process that brought me to consider how limiting for myself and discriminatory vis-à-vis others it was to uphold such a demanding aesthetic benchmark. Because Belgium, this tiny, pleasant and welcoming country in the heart of Europe, doesn't care much about aesthetics, at least in the classical sense. Belgium is one of the world's cradles of the grotesque. If you don't have time to become acquainted with its painters, performing artists, and films, just consider that the symbol of Brussels, its capital city, is the statue of a little boy peeing—on the burning fuse of the explosive charge that was about to destroy the city, as the legend goes. I have not come across any other country or city sporting a similarly humorous and mischievous symbol. Have you?

Coming to daily habits, the people walking around the city cover the entire spectrum of clothing possibilities, from pajamas to black tie, the vast majority being dressed in understated colors, forms, and shapes. Moreover, it is perfectly normal for a person to water their front garden flowers in a dressing gown, something that would be perceived as totally inappropriate behavior in Italy. And nobody will raise an eyebrow if you happen to be walking in public at 10:00 in the morning wrapped in a black garbage bag. The idea being that you could have a good reason for that—say, a fancy dress party for early birds—which do not necessarily involve crime or evildoing, so why bother?

While at the beginning I looked down on Belgian inhabitants, as they didn't seem as concerned about elegance as Italians, very quickly I realized that this new context would enable me to start wearing more comfortable clothes and shoes. I had never bought hiking trousers and sports sandals up until then, would you believe it? Belgium also freed me from the need to follow seasonal fashion changes, which would have been a top priority in Italy for a young career woman like me. I finally realized that fashion is a contradiction in terms: how could the same trendy shapes and colors possibly make every woman the most beautiful version of herself, knowing how different we all are? Yet, in my country of origin being out of fashion meant you sucked, so much so that even poorer parts of the population used to strive to find cheap copies of fashionable clothes. And this was true for both women and men, even though for the latter the fashion markers were less conspicuous than for women.

There was an element, though, that predisposed me to develop a more critical view of fashion and body image: being a feminist from an early age, I hated the fact that women were spotlighted as attractive, luring objects on billboards, on TV, in magazines, and at popular events. I found this disgraceful, unfair, and profoundly discriminatory. This meant that the foundations for my questioning the influence of Italian mainstream image and bodily norms had been laid down inside me since I was a child. And they rested on fundamental values like justice and equality.

Interestingly enough, from such composite roots I developed a very personal ideal that put elegance and physical beauty very high on the scale of the professional skills I aspired to possess. My view was that, to serve Europe and to perform at the highest level, I needed to give the best possible image of myself. Due to the influence that Belgium was exerting on me though, I devised a sort of double standard, always very elegant in the office but giving priority to comfort and ease when it came to choosing my clothes for leisure time. Without being completely aware of the transformation of my perceptions, I was starting to experience and enjoy some freedom in the way I related to my image. And for this I will always be grateful to Belgium.

My path to freeing myself from image beliefs and constraints was still steep and long, though. In 2001, when I was stepping up as a team leader in a critical coordination role in my organization, a small private incident brought to my attention the contradictions inherent in the professional image of a woman.

Due to my busy work schedule and my husband's academic and artistic activities, we had entrusted the afterschool care of our children, aged five and three, to a lovely Belgian lady of Cambodian descent in her mid-forties. She picked them up from school at three-thirty, accompanied them to their afternoon's activities and helped them do their homework until six-thirty, when I came back from work. She was exquisitely elegant, and on top of that her skin, make-up, and nails were always flawless. She had two lovely daughters in their pre-teens, and one day she happened to come around with the elder girl. When I came back home from the office, the little girl looked at me in awe and cried, "You look so beautiful and smart! You must be a secretary!"

Her mom, who knew that actually I had secretaries working for me, felt very embarrassed and apologized for her, "So sorry Madam, she thinks so highly of secretaries that she cannot imagine a better job than that."

Of course, I smiled and replied that she should not worry, I understood that was a sincere compliment, and I was receiving it as such. But later I could not deny being saddened by the girl's remark, as it was shedding a new light on the way I could be perceived outside my workplace. Not only was the "very important" role I had in my organization a mystery to most of humankind, but the priority I attached to my physical looks could actually "demote" me to less prestigious jobs in the eyes of people with different backgrounds. What I was experiencing was shame—in other terms the feeling of being not enough, being wrong, unworthy. That did not happen often to me because shame, as Chris

Germer powerfully puts it[13], comes from the innocent wish to be loved. A wish that emerges at birth: without love, care, and attention, babies would die. Psychology and evolutionary theory converge here to clarify why the emotion of shame has developed: to make sure we survive. The other side of the coin is that shame is so tenacious and secretive that often we are not even aware of it. And getting to befriend it requires us to cultivate self-awareness and self-compassion.

I was generally shielded from shame by the awareness that I was loved unconditionally, certainly by God, my husband, my children, and my parents. However, shame had found its way into me through the channel of my image, because, at least in the eyes of our babysitter's daughter, I was not recognizable for who I was professionally, no matter how much effort I put into showing up as well-groomed and aesthetically polished as I could. A bit like the Evil Queen in front of her Magic Mirror.

I decided to give some thought to the fact that a well-intended compliment had revealed something profound about the way I related to my public image. Which was not easy and straight-forward, but contained different angles and layers of meaning. One of my learning points was that granting so much importance to my image did not necessarily fit well with my professional ambition. I started wondering whether it could even play against my career chances. Maybe I would need to choose between the two at some point, to show which mattered more to me? I was

---

[13] Chris Germer, *What's behind shame? An innocent wish to be loved.* YouTube, video, 11:27, posted by Stan Steindl, February 16, 2024, https://www.youtube.com/watch?v=55HPOw9nQ8s&list=PLroO7mpqhnSe07vXi-wuX-DGmBEU3EI2jh&index=4.

starting to wonder whether people in general, and colleagues of mine in particular, might interpret my attention to elegance as a sign that I was not putting work first. I found those doubts quite upsetting, because I firmly believed that elegance came naturally to me. I wouldn't have known where to start if I had to show up in less smart clothes at the office.

At that time I was not even scratching the surface of a much more fundamental issue. The role of elegance in my life was actually the result of a deeply ingrained creed. The creed that, to consider myself worthy, I needed to look good and classy. Against this background, was it even possible for me to reconnect with my genuine preferences about image? And how could I distance myself from the power that the judgment of others exerted on me? Because for sure, every day, when I came back from work, I immediately switched from precious outfits to track pants or night gowns. When I was in the safe space of my house, I could feel free and well only in loose and casual clothes, the older the better.

The same happened with my contact lenses: I had never spent more than five minutes with them on at home. In the privacy of my house I always wore glasses, even though I would rather put on a burqa than show myself wearing glasses at work or public events. This last self-limitation was essentially due to my severe myopia and the fact that my eyes looked incredibly small behind my thick glasses, but even so: wasn't this kind of choice—again—proof that it was difficult for me to accept my natural appearance, because of how others might assess it?

My awareness of the exaggerated importance I had given to my public image and looks required decades to emerge. It took another embarrassing situation of image-related shame in 2007 for me to accelerate my inner learning curve. This situation caused me nightmares until a few years ago. Its memory has faded over time, becoming the most precise indicator of my liberation from the grip of image. Indeed, since I started befriending self-compassion, merely remembering this episode has decreased my negative emotions, and today I am even capable of laughing about it. But please believe me, this is no small feat knowing where I was coming from.

Back in 2007 I was still in the cabinet of Mr Figel', the European Commissioner responsible for Education and Culture. He had been invited to several events in Milan. This included appearing as guest of honor at a performance of *Così fan tutte*, the witty opera about love and gender roles composed by Mozart. This was scheduled at La Scala, Milan's opera house, in the autumn of that year. Being the only Italian member of the cabinet, I usually accompanied my Commissioner on his business trips to Italy, and I jumped with joy when his personal assistant broke the news to me. Going to La Scala was one of my secret dreams: the historic opera house was the cradle and the world stage of *bel canto* and the most famous Italian operas, and we Italians worship opera singers. I prepared with great care for that memorable event, packing a very elegant silk black dress that suited me perfectly in my cabin luggage.

I should have felt that something was wrong the moment that, for the first (and so far only) time in my life, I missed my plane. It was due to a series of unfortunate circumstances, because I was so eager to take off that I had arrived at the airport three hours before the plane departure. Possibly too early, because the gate changed at the last moment and I realized it too late, as I was on the phone. Luckily, I was rerouted on another flight that was set to land in Milan minutes before the Commissioner's, who was travelling from Slovakia. So, all was still fine from a professional point of view, in spite of my delay. In hindsight, catching the earlier flight would have provided ample time for me to solve the wicked problem I was confronted with later that day. Anyway, the Commissioner and I jumped into the official car that had been sent to pick us up and drop us at the hotel for just 15 minutes before taking us to the opera house.

Now we come to the crunch (be compassionate, please don't laugh): as soon as I locked the door of my hotel room, I extracted my little black dress from my cabin luggage. What emerged was a total wreck of a dress, full of wrinkles and looking like a rag. I was desperate and could not gather my thoughts. I just wanted to disappear. I quickly realized that I had no time to have it ironed at the hotel. I desperately tried to iron it out with my hands, with no success. Truth is that my dress was always impeccable hanging in my closet at home, and I had never packed it before, so I had no idea that this particular cloth would get so creased and wrinkled in a carry-on bag.

I hated myself for having been unable to see the disaster coming. I would have hated myself more if I had known that actually the best way to pack any clothes is to roll them instead of folding them. This simple trick would have pre-empted the issue altogether—so that you know, just in case you are as sensitive to wrinkled clothes as I am. I was going to call the hotel housekeeper and confess my shameful situation when I received a text from the Commissioner saying that he was ready and waiting for me downstairs. Sense of duty prevailed, and in total despair I took a standard-sized briefing file out of my suitcase and decided to keep it tightly in front of me anytime I would be standing, to hide at least some of the disgraceful creases. You know, a bit like Meg in *Little Women* (chapter 3) by L. M. Alcott, when she realizes, right before leaving with her sister Jo for the New Year's Eve party at Mrs. Gardiner's, that her sister's gloves are stained. No way could they be perceived as well-bred girls at such a posh reception without gloves! So, in the end they decide to wear each one of Meg's good pair of gloves, and crumple one of Jo's stained ones in the other hand. Still, I would have gladly exchanged my problem with theirs, as hiding the creases of a whole dress with a briefing file seemed to me much more desperate.

During the ride from the hotel to La Scala, while the Commissioner was cheerily expressing his interest in opera, I could only think about the state of my poor dress and the fact that I was going to lose face in one of the temples of Italian elegance: it is a well-known fact in Italy that the performances at La Scala attract a very elegant crowd. And I was accompanying my Commissioner, the guest of honor! I was going to disgrace not only me as a person, but as a high-placed Italian civil servant in Europe. Shame for my country and shame for my employer!

The 20 minutes spent in the car provided a much-needed truce for my emotions. What happened next made me feel like Cersei during her famous walk of shame (*Game of Thrones*, season 5, episode 10). I stepped out of the car and there they stood, the members of the welcoming committee. All women! I would have hoped for some gender balance, as men, even when they happen to be Italian, are notoriously less used to realizing the real magnitude of a total fashion failure—this is how pitilessly I judged myself that evening. I was certain that the ladies in front of me were noticing, counting, and classifying every single crease, wrinkle, or otherwise imperfect spot on my dress. Of course, they were showing exquisite politeness both to the Commissioner and myself, which made me feel even more ashamed.

I could find solace only in the compassionately dark embrace of the Royal Loggia in La Scala, sitting behind the Commissioner, because there nobody could notice the state of my dress. During the pauses, the cocktail and the interviews that followed I stood stoically behind my briefing file, praying that people would not look at me, secretly yelling at my stupidity and unworthiness with words that were the exact contrary of compassion, like "how could you be such an idiot?", "what will these people think of you?", "how could you disgrace yourself and everything you represent like this?"—and I am transcribing here only the kinder insults among those I invented for myself on that fateful day.

Of course, I have no proof that the people I met that evening noticed my dress's pitiful state. Possibly they had, each and all, their own issues or reasons to think about something else. But even if one, or more, of the Italians we met did notice and assess my elegance level as poor, what would have been the problem? Would that have changed my life? Here I hold the answer: it clearly wouldn't have, and didn't. My perceived fashion catastrophe bore absolutely no consequence on my professional life. A conclusion that deserves meditating on!

When, the following year, I went back to La Scala and represented my organization in an impeccable, gorgeous cocktail dress that did not need any ironing, I was worried that somebody might remember my previous shameful appearance and still judge me negatively because of it. How silly of me! As if anyone could really stay hooked for one full year onto something that crosses their path by pure chance and is of no consequence to them. Just try it out for yourself: I am ready to bet that you could not remember anything similar that happened last week, let alone one year ago, even if you are very sensitive to elegance and cloth wrinkles.

Slowly but surely, since 2007 the way I relate to my image has taken a wiser turn and led me to experience more and more freedom in the way I perceive my physical appearance, progressively nudging me into a much more relaxed approach to elegance. Elegance for me has become a choice instead of a suffocating obligation, and this has increased my degree of freedom and considerably improved my quality of life.

In parallel, I was—inevitably—growing older. I was managing to factor in my age in a way that was more helpful than shameful: I have always thought that getting older is a victory, rather than an unwelcome development in life. Yet, I had still not come to the point that I could imagine myself as both old and beautiful. I was rather clinging to the illusion that my fair complexion and my wild curls would keep me looking forever young. I surely never thought that one day I would make a statement out of aging. But in the end, why not? Nobody can stay forever young. How old do you have to be to accept that every day adds on the previous one? How many thousands of days does it take to realize that aging can become an embodiment of humility too; one day more or less cannot change our worth in any way? And to realize that young and old are not the most meaningful words to describe our being. Still, my desire to find myself as beautiful as ever was a fierce drag on my inner growth.

So, when I finally made peace with my difficult decision to stop dyeing my hair, allowing amazing black-and-white curls to emerge, I realized it was a true blessing. Everybody liked my new look, which helped me keep a reasonable level of self-appreciation, and nobody could tell my age anymore by looking at my face—not even me! Actually, I realized that I had broken the mold in which beauty equated a young, slim, agreeably faced, and non-gray person. People would see my face, which still looks relatively young for my age, together with my salt-and-pepper hair, and would be so surprised that they would not even think of how old I was, but simply concentrate on the human being who stood in front of them. So, aging unexpectedly became a much more natural fact of life to me once I stopped dyeing my hair.

However, another element was going to emerge out of my growth and my coming to terms with aging. This, little by little, led me to conceive beauty as the expression of inner light more than the result of desirable physical features.

Accepting myself as I was led me to feel that my poor body had been storing and piling up all the suffering, pain, and sorrow I had gone through during many years, meaning my professional setbacks, my disappointment and frustration at not succeeding in getting a good job outside my organization, and the ordeal of the COVID-19 pandemic. Something that you cannot even notice while you are frantically trying to look different from who you are. It took somebody named Tenzin to unravel it.

In 2020, during one of my weekly coaching sessions with Helen, I uttered a little moan coming from tension in my shoulder blades. Soon after, Helen dropped a casual sentence about a wonderful Tibetan lady who was able to give the most powerful and effective traditional massage she had ever experienced.

"I would really recommend that you fix an appointment with her. Her place is far from luxurious and her prices are extremely reasonable compared to what you can find in Brussels, but I have never enjoyed better quality Tibetan massages."

I took Helen at her word. She certainly knew what she was talking about, having been a Buddhist nun in Asia for a few months, and I valued her advice highly. So off I went immediately after our coaching video call, texting Tenzin (the masseuse's name) to request an appointment.

The "Tibetan Health Center", as the massage place was pompously called on its webpage, was an unassuming back shop located in a popular neighborhood of Brussels. Helen's recommendation was enough to make me feel immediately at ease in a place that I would possibly otherwise never have tried out. It's revealing how we are generally more willing to trust shops and places based just on their luxurious appearance! I also liked the smell of incense that welcomed me, before noticing the broad smile in Tenzin's eyes; the pandemic was still forcing us to hide the rest of our faces under surgical masks. She led me gently to one of the very simple but warm individual cabins where the massages took place. She let me in, gave me a couple of minutes to undress and lie face down on the massage bed and came back, ready to start.

She found my first name very cute and explained that Tenzin was the first name of the Dalai Lama. For this reason many Tibetan people, both men and women, were given that name. She asked me whether I would like a gentle, medium, or strong massage, and I told her to do what she thought best, as it was the first time in my life that I was getting a traditional Tibetan massage. She went for a medium-intensity massage, but I experienced it as very strong. Very soon I started feeling waves of pain emerging and dissipating all along and across my body, whenever her hands found my muscles, tendons, and nerves. I wept the entire hour that the massage lasted, while at the same time being drawn to talk about life and wisdom with her.

Tenzin was surprised by the amount of tension and pain entrapped in my body: not one single muscle seemed to be free from either of them. She regularly inquired whether I could take any more, and I kept on replying positively while sobbing my tensions away. I could follow her movements circling on my back, going down my spine like electric dolphins, laboring my thighs, knees, and ankles as if they were a dry and rocky field. The entire experience was extremely painful, yet I could bear with it because, just after the peaks of pain, I felt a sense of relief that I could not compare to anything I had experienced before. I understood later that her massage had embodied my compassion for all the sorrows and the shame that had stiffened and twisted my body over the years.

When she completed the massage, she brought me scalding wet towels that landed like a balm on my skin and sore muscles. She comforted me, gently asking how it felt now, and I murmured, "Like liberation." She recommended that I do some stretching, even only 10 minutes a day, at least four or five times a week, to make sure I would never again find myself in a similar situation of compounded stress, tension, and suffering. And she suggested that I come back for a massage at least once every two months, to prevent the body from tensing so much that release and relaxing it would again require lots of pain.

My first encounter with Tenzin was definitely one of those turning points in life that teach you something that cannot be unlearned. Body and mind are so deeply interconnected that there is no way that mental suffering would not imprint itself on the body one way or the other. I suddenly realized that I had been paying much more attention and offered many more hours of care to my skin than to what lay beneath. I had come to a point where I had to undertake sustained, regular, and compassionate action if I wanted to preserve my ability to move smoothly with no or hardly any pain.

I was literally dropping inside my body to understand its basic needs and cater for them, probably for the first time since I was a baby. I also knew that the hour I had spent in pain under the magical hands of Tenzin, who had spared no effort or energy to free me from suffering, was the entry door into dimensions of my life I had very much underestimated so far. Aging meant that I could not continue walking the path of youth without putting my health at risk. I realized how this increased awareness was bringing something more into my life. How wisdom was filling the space left behind by youth. I felt that my sense of happiness could expand on new grounds and make my whole life experience fuller and more meaningful. And I felt more thankful than ever to Helen, who had so wisely offered me this new gift.

Then, a couple of years later, I had a call with a Stanford student, a soon-to-be Ambassador of Applied Compassion, to discuss one-on-one about some results emerging from her Capstone project, a very interesting survey on connection and distress when working with remote teams. Actually, I had been bubbling with excitement for a couple of days, because I knew we would be discussing compassion in the workplace, my purpose since 2021. Her LinkedIn profile described her as an experienced professional coach and leadership teacher. When she appeared on Zoom, I liked her immediately: her energy, her way of speaking, clear and direct, the quality of her inquiries, and the sincerity of her heart. More than that: she came with something I had not anticipated. After just one or two minutes online, she cried out, "You have the most beautiful smile I have ever seen. Can I call you from time to time, just to see it more often?"

At the beginning, I was so surprised that I did not know how to react. Then I managed to welcome with gratitude that spontaneous manifestation of warm human connection, and I replied, "Thank you for saying so, it is a gift to me."

I recalled that many people, all along my life, had been expressing appreciation for my smile, its glow, its warmth, its outreach. Already when I was a baby my smile would soothe many of the adults around me, and attract other children. Then came my "existential crisis"—you will learn more about this later—when I was six years old, that deprived me of my smile for two years. Then, when I was eight, smiles came back to be my faithful companions, without interruption. It was only when I was around 40, however, that I realized that smiling as a way of being was not that widespread, and more and more people were telling me that they liked my smile. Needless to say, for someone used to assessing beauty, in myself as well as in others, that was likely to mean "they tell you this more often now because they cannot honestly say that you are beautiful anymore". So wrong, and so petty of me. As if beauty could exist only while we are young! Not to mention how everything gets richer when we interpret others' behaviors generously, in ways that nourish compassion.

Yet again, I was painfully climbing my wisdom learning curve. Little by little, I came to consider that, maybe, a smiling face can be more uplifting than a beautiful one, also because the love and warmth expressed by a smile does not age, contrary to skin and face. And finally, I completely reversed my approach, coming to believe that, while physical beauty can only be preserved up to a certain point and then inevitably wears away because of aging, suffering, and sickness, smiling can always be a part of us and shared at any age. Moreover, smiling expresses beauty in a much more profound way than a juvenile face and body can. Which, in the end, means that ageless, inner beauty is available to everyone, because it does not depend on aesthetics, but on our degree of wisdom and eudemonic happiness: I refer here to a state of happiness that is lasting and meaningful because it is steeped in purpose and can coexist with pain and suffering.

There was certainly a part of me that grew up believing, like the Evil Queen, that one of the top priorities in life for any woman, and even more for those holding professional responsibilities, was to be regarded as the most beautiful, elegant, and fit. My experiences revealed to me how compelling and intimidating the eyes of others could be in this context—both for women and men, even though in different ways. This weighed on my life for a very long time and prevented me from aligning my image with my being. Only in these last few years did I manage to evolve from a very constraining and unfair duty to express feminine beauty at any public appearance to the acceptance of aging as a phase in life where inner wisdom can be perceived as beautiful in surprising ways, like my ageless smile and my white curls.

Among the insights that helped me grow was the following consideration: what if the others' judgment only had the power we give it, or let it have? Of course, I am not saying we can—or should—live simply ignoring the opinion of others on anything, including on our appearance. Nor that we should never align with it. However, the final decision on how to appear, what to wear and how to deal with our body belongs to us. Understanding and embodying this freedom can dramatically improve our chances of feeling happy over time. Self-compassion has much to bring in this context, too, as the path is long, rocky, and winding: being our own best friend when we feel miserable or unworthy is an incredible source of resilience and hope. And it will help us try on those outfits that we have always dreamt about but never dared wear!

All in all, the journey that has led me to drop the Evil Queen's Magic Mirror has enabled me to understand and overcome shame through self-compassion—and deepen my freedom. My way of showing up in the world is now rooted in my being, not in my naive over-confidence or in a pre-cooked conception of beauty as a feminine duty. I am aware of what other people may think of my appearance. But the awareness of how my appearance may be judged by others does not limit my choices and my style anymore. For example, gone is my habit to always show up in a jacket at the office, the signature of any "decent" career woman. Conversely, I have (almost) lost my Italian habit of judging people on the basis of how they appear. Actually, I now devote the amount of attention and energy liberated by this fundamental change in my attitude to really get to know people as they are.

And trust me, they deserve it!

To summarize and help you practice, through meditation, journaling, or self-reflection, I have listed here the self-inquiry questions underpinning chapter 9:

- Can I describe how I relate to my natural appearance? If I could rediscover my genuine preferences, how would I show up in public?

- How could I distance myself from the impact that the judgment of others has on how I see myself? If I can imagine taking even just a baby step in that direction, to start with, what would that step be?

- Have I ever said to myself: "How could you be such an idiot?", "What will these people think of you?", or something similar? If yes, in which circumstances? What would a more skillful reaction in that situation look like?

- Can I recall a situation where I felt ashamed? How did it manifest itself in my body? Do my bodily sensations shift or change if I treat myself like a very good friend would do?

- Can one day more or one day less in my life change my worth in any way? Why?

- What do I fear would happen to me if I dropped the Evil Queen's Magic Mirror and stopped criticizing myself for my body image? How could I address those fears or worries?

What It Takes to Be Yourself

And you can add your own self-inquiry questions below:

_____

_____

_____

_____

Finally, I have selected a resource for you that I find very powerful in connection with this chapter, a powerful quote by Ralph Waldo Emerson, from *Culture, Beauty, Behavior:* "There is no beautifier of complexion, or form, or behavior, like the wish to scatter joy and not pain around us."

For more, don't hesitate to browse through my "Recommended Resources" at the end of the book.

CHAPTER TEN

Approaching Money through the Lens of Triggers

Zombie, The Cranberries

Money, money, money. It's not only a global hit by Abba. It's something difficult to define, and it has many facets. It is a value to some, an obstacle to others. Many crave it, long for it, some even kill for it. Others may believe that it is a proof of personal worth, or that it is the prerequisite for happiness. My personal relationship to money has been evolving over five decades, and it has often proven complicated. For this reason, I'll be honest with you, I wondered whether I should even write a chapter about money. I felt it as an unpleasant obligation. But could I really pretend to write a book addressing the meaning of success and never touch upon money? And yet, I tried to wriggle my way out of it for two years.

In the end, I decided that yes, I would write a chapter where money plays a role, but no, this chapter would not be about money as a component of success. First of all, because this is obvious to a majority of people almost everywhere in the world. Secondly, because while exploring this topic I realized that our personal relationship to money often encapsulates powerful triggers. Nobody is free from triggers, and they can make us feel truly miserable. Worse: they can block our access to compassion. For this reason, addressing triggers skillfully was one of the key teachings of my Applied Compassion Training. That's the angle I will adopt to address money here. Because I'm ready to bet that most of us have issues when it comes to it.

Triggers are a specific set of issues that can be defined as upsetting, unexpected emotional reactions set off by a word, person, event, or experience. Triggers are challenging because they are cues that involuntarily recall past traumatic experiences. Because of this connection, when we learn to approach them in a way that decreases their intensity and helps us understand their deeper connection into our human experience, they can offer valuable opportunities to cultivate compassion for us and others. And learning to address them skillfully opens the door to deeper healing, helps us to grow, and eases our path toward happiness. I will share a couple of difficult personal experiences related to money that have taught me much about triggers and what they can reveal, hoping that this may resonate with you and help you navigate your triggers with money—or anything else.

I am lucky enough to have never experienced a situation where I had no money at all. So, I can certainly relate to a Chinese proverb, "Money is no problem. The problem is no money". It was written in red, capital letters on a black T-shirt that I brought to my son from my first business trip to China. I guess that, apart from St. Francis, who gave up a life of privilege and wealth to live on people's generosity until his death, few other people would disagree with it.

However, if I take a closer look at this proverb, I realize that I have my doubts about its first half. "Money is no problem", really? We all wish to have money in order to have enough to drink and eat, to buy clothes, to enjoy a roof on our head, and a series of things that help us feel safe, healthy, and possibly happy. However, money is not enough to fulfill our every need and wish. Researchers in this area recently found out that earning more money increases people's happiness—but only up to $75,000 USD per year (in the US). Once we hit that figure, we are more likely to increase our happiness by adding 20 minutes to our sleeping time than by earning more money[14]. So, it looks like money may always be a problem, either because we don't have enough of it, or because it does not suffice to make us happy. My personal experience is that I have struggled greatly to develop a reasonably balanced relationship to money, just like many people I know. And you, my dear reader, how would you describe your relationship to money?

The other important caveat I need to mention here is that in Europe we do not talk easily of money. Generally we don't ask somebody how

---

[14] Laurie Santos, "Here's How Much Money You Need to Be Happy," YouTube video, posted by Yale University, September 13, 2019, https://www.youtube.com/watch?v=iRzjBBNRufg.

much they earn, unless they are part of the family, or we have a very specific reason for asking. Even so, it often takes guts to feel allowed or entitled to inquire, and a negative, embarrassed, or elusive answer can rarely be ruled out. As if money were a part of our intimacy. Something really important, but that we do not show easily.

At the same time, money should not be wasted, right? As usual, the devil is in the detail, because the thin frontier that separates what is reasonable spending from what is foolish, or even inordinate, spending is left to our discretion. I still remember my mother worrying about my possible stinginess when she saw how I managed my weekly pocket money as a young girl. It's true that I was too wary of using it in a way that would attract negative judgment on me. If I bought h or desserts I would be called a glutton, and sweet treats were bad for my physical shape (from age 8 to 14 I was quite puffy). Buying books would be judged as a superfluous act, because we had hundreds of them at home that I had not read yet. And that was pretty much all, because I was a dutiful girl who would wait for Christmas or the seasonal sales before asking for clothes or toys and would let her parents choose what was best for her.

So, already at a tender age, I learned to limit my wishes to what I considered to be reasonable and necessary. I would never buy anything unless I was absolutely certain that I needed it, that I liked it, and that it suited me well. I became addicted to price reductions, special offers, and the like. I would go a fair distance to find an alternative to a product or service if I believed it was too expensive, including parking fees once I started driving. I developed a personal theory that linked prices with justice, which made me feel cheated or betrayed whenever I realized I had paid more than the usual price for something. These habits turned me into an incredibly efficient spender and effective organizer. However, they also built constraints and boundaries inside me that I was barely aware of.

When I moved to Belgium and met Serge, I could immediately see that his relation to money was quite different from mine. He would not blink when buying expensive gifts (especially if they were intended for me or for good friends) or books, while he had other sorts of money allergies. For example, he would not spend much on clothes—what was the point anyway in a country like Belgium, where it is easy to show up at the opera house in anything ranging from track pants to tuxedo? Track pants cost less and are much more comfortable, so cheap clothes in limited quantities were clearly the choice of the majority, and a no-brainer compared to my complicated calculations prior to every purchase.

You remember that with my demanding Italian background I could not easily give up on fashion and a conspicuous number of elegant clothes. So, once in Brussels, I enthusiastically embraced thrift shops, which were a total novelty to me and enabled me to discover hidden gems for a fraction of the original tag price. This habit came with an unwanted consequence: over the years, I became accustomed to seeking bargains, so much so that I would not even think of buying something just because I liked it. More recently, I have decided to train myself to do so in the name of freedom, and I am glad to report that it has become a conscious choice, now close to coming naturally to me.

Serge and I learned from each other and jointly developed a more balanced relationship to spending money. Going to gastronomic restaurants became little by little one of our favorite ways to celebrate anniversaries, successes, and milestones. I was not used at all to enjoying "real" restaurants, because when I was younger my friends and I could only afford pizzas or ice cream parlors.

The result was that we decided to innovate: we became restaurant explorers. At the beginning, I still hesitated before ordering a dish that featured among the most expensive ones on the menu. Little by little I got used to focusing on the food experience and things improved. Today I can enjoy excellent food to celebrate something important with my loved ones without giving a thought to the final bill.

Another sort of pleasure that requires money is jewelry. I have always loved the beauty and the spark of precious stones and noble metals, helped by the fact that the Italian culture I was brought up in allows, better, requires every family, even the poorest, to invest money in luscious jewelry for every milestone in life—basically birth, baptism, First Communion, wedding, and when possible, birthdays and anniversaries too. It's both a love statement and a very good investment, so here popular wisdom goes hand in hand with sound budget management. However, the conjunction of my love for luxury goods and my fear of spending unwisely can unleash strong triggers. Let me share a recent one with you, a story which shows that we never stop learning, even when we start to believe that we have found the path to wisdom.

As I said, I have a taste for jewels. This includes precious watches. I like silver very much, but until recently I did not own any silver watches. I wanted to fill the gap, so I started consulting the webpages of a second-hand watch shop where I had already bought two vintage gold watches to my great satisfaction. One day, while I was connecting to the page, a pop-up window appeared, informing the internet users that the shop would close soon, and for this reason most watches came with huge price cuts. My heart jumped with joy, as nothing seemed sweeter to me than acquiring a luxury watch at half price. Moreover, I was considering buying a lovely Jaeger LeCoultre watch, a rare Swiss-made beauty with an ornate bracelet, all made of silver, which was luring me from the website. I immediately reached out to the retailer on WhatsApp, asking for the final price. He swiftly replied quoting a very interesting amount, which represented only 40% of the original price. I went to the shop, tried it on and noticed with disappointment that the bracelet was way too long for my wrist. The seller, who seemed to be a decent man and a real expert in watches, immediately proposed to cut two of the links that formed the bracelet to make it fit my wrist perfectly, and we concluded the deal for the bargain price. I gave him almost half of the amount as a down payment without blinking and came out of the shop feeling euphoric, exhilarated, and proud of the unique, bespoke, amazing object that would soon be in my possession.

However, not only did the seller not come back to me as promptly as I had expected, but some weeks later he sent me a bizarre email, asking whether I would agree to pay for the "repair". I immediately reacted from a place of anger ("Why is he changing the terms of the contract? Does he want to make fun of me, or worse, to scam me?") and fear ("Oh my goodness, he has my phone number and my email address, maybe he's planning even worse things than keeping both my advance payment and my watch!"). Happily, I quickly realized that I had been abundantly triggered by the situation, and before replying fierily I went to Serge to tap into his wisdom. Contrary to me, he remained calm. He found the situation funny (which, to tell the truth, did not land well with me), and helped me draft a factual, dry reply.

My heart was beating like crazy when I clicked on the "send" icon. Three hours—and lots of sweating—later, the seller replied that "OK, then I will do it for free". Serge seemed satisfied with the reply, while I continued ruminating and worrying that he might want to play cat and mouse with me, silently yelling at myself for being such a lame customer in spite of being recognized as a world-class expert in consumer protection—self-compassion, where were you in those moments? What made me really anxious was that whenever I texted him, politely asking when I could go and collect my watch, he simply replied that it was not ready yet. True, he had hinted at the fact that the specialist who carried out repairs for him had left on a long holiday, but I was irresistibly attracted by more dramatic hypotheses, all leading to a scary finale where I would lose both my money and my watch.

My worries skyrocketed when I read on his website (yes, I admit I was regularly checking the shop website, to be sure he would not put my watch up again for sale) a pop-up note saying that he was closing down the shop and soon would only operate from a private office. I started imagining that he was doing so because he wanted to scam several customers: if the shop disappeared, how could anyone possibly trace him back? He might just leave the country forever. I suddenly remembered that he had talked about Moroccan jewelry as another of his specialties.

So, my fertile imagination pictured him in Casablanca, like a modern adventurer in the steps of Humphrey Bogart.

My doubts became a certainty in my mind when I saw the picture of my watch pop up again on the website (which had not disappeared, by the way) without any price tag: I took this as a proof of the looming scam.

Right then, I received an email from him, informing me that the watch was ready.

I was completely torn inside. Half of me was dead scared that the man would try to bring me to a private place to perform God knows what crime. The other half was lighting up and believing that there was a solid chance I would finally—and safely—get my watch. Serge, of course, was convinced of the latter, and even more so when the seller texted me to explain that his shop had closed down and we could meet whenever and wherever I proposed, provided it was not too far from the area of Brussels he lived in. He also asked for cash, as his credit card reader did not function. Creepy, I immediately thought.

Like a replica of the autistic protagonist of *Monk*, a detective TV series from 2002, I decided to choose a public, open-air place, where it would be easy for me to escape in case he displayed any aggressive behavior, or tried to snatch my cash and flee with it, or worse. So, I suggested that we meet a Saturday afternoon at a well-known Brussels monumental cemetery—yes, of all things! —not far from where he lived.

That day we were blessed with beautiful weather and pleasant temperatures. I arrived at the cemetery gate and stood there for one minute, my heart racing, feeling the envelope where I had put the money through the fabric of my jacket and calling myself names for taking the risk of a potential robbery. Right then I sighted him on the other side of the street. He waved his hand, clearly suggesting that I come to him. I reluctantly crossed the street, reckoning that he couldn't do anything bad in public. He shook my hand and amicably offered to go for coffee at a nearby place. That was the very moment my heartbeat started calming down. I explained that I was in a hurry (which was true) and that we could do the "exchange" ("Is it even legal to complete a sale on the street?" my inner voice was wondering at the same time) sitting on a bench of the cemetery. He followed me obediently, another reassuring fact and, as soon as we sat down, he reached for his pocket and showed the watch to me. It was so beautiful, shining its silvery light under the sun! Every doubt melted away when he put it around my wrist, explaining, like only an expert who sincerely loves what he does can do, how to take care of it, how to wind it, how to clean it, and so on. I was flabbergasted. I also reached for my pocket, extracted the envelope and handed it to him.

"Please do count it, just to be sure I did not make any mistake."

He smiled and said that he trusted me, there was no need to count. He also insisted that he was available if I ever encountered any problem with the watch. He went on, sharing that he had a real passion for watches and would continue to buy vintage ones and resell them, so if I was looking for something in particular I could always tell him, as he remained at my disposal. We even hugged at the end.

The last surprise linked to the story of the watch knocked on my heart a couple of hours later. I was back home and I was projecting again in my mind what had happened that afternoon. I had a slight doubt about the sum that was left to be paid, and I realized that I had paid 10 euros less than the agreed price. I felt really bad, as I was now in the shoes of an unintentional scammer—and what a ludicrous one, on top of everything! But he never called me back to reclaim the missing amount.

I was taken aback. For almost two months I had been imagining all sorts of painful scenarios that only happened in my head, like in the famous quip by Mark Twain: "I've lived through some terrible things in my life, some of which actually happened". In the end, I got everything I wanted exactly as it had been agreed with the seller. Actually, even a tiny bit less expensively. Sure, the purchase did not happen in a normal shop and it felt awkward to exchange a beautiful object against the balance in cash while sitting on a cemetery bench. It would have probably felt suspicious if the weather had been less glorious, but that's not the point.

Truth is that I made a lot of fuss, and suffered quite a lot from it, not because what I feared was real but because I mistook my fear for the reality. I accepted that the whole watch situation had strongly triggered me and I decided to work on it, using a very powerful exercise about triggers that I received as a lasting gift from my teachers at Stanford. This self-reflective practice has proven very effective every time I have used it to uncover my triggers. I will call it "the seven whys". It is a self-inquiry with a simple structure that takes you seven levels down inside your conscience, a bit like when you stand between two mirrors, one facing you and the other one behind you, and the same image is reflected ad infinitum in both mirrors. Happily for us, a seven-story self-inquiry into the depth of our heart is generally more than enough to get to the hurtful memories awakened by our triggers.

How does it work concretely? You start by asking yourself: why was I triggered in this situation? Then you continue by asking why—up to seven times—like a little child. Let's apply it to my example:

1. why was I triggered in the silver watch situation? Because I thought that the seller wanted to take advantage of me.
2. And why did I think that? Because if somebody takes advantage of me, I feel like a fool, I judge myself as not being clever enough, and I don't like this feeling.
3. Why do I want to avoid feeling that way? Because it means others will assume I am not clever enough. I am not showing up the way I am. And I start being very critical of myself.
4. Why would I start criticizing myself? Because I repeat the behavior of my mother when I was harassed at school. When I told her she said she did not want to hear anything about this ever again.
5. Why do I inflict this behavior on myself? Because it is the only way not to recall and face what happened to me when I was eight: the pain, the suffering and the humiliation, the injustice and the racism, the trauma and the loneliness I experienced as a little kid.

So after only five "whys" I managed to highlight the old wound that the trigger was covertly reconnecting to. I am convinced that I managed to do this self-inquiry relatively easily just because the hypnosis experience had already succeeded in overturning the memories of my childhood trauma, so that this related trigger did not need to protect me as fiercely as before. In my experience, and for many of my Applied Compassion Training fellow students too, the roots of triggers are generally difficult to unmask and require much more patience, and repeated self-inquiries.

However, the exercise of the seven whys can lead us gently into the layered levels of our past, helping us to discover a bit more about them with every "why?"

When I practice this self-inquiry and feel I am hitting a wall inside myself, I just take note of where I have got to, and the next time it feels OK to continue digging I start from there. I really recommend this practice because, even when you know that there is something deeper left to discover, you already feel relieved for becoming aware of a little bit, which can shed light on any recurring strong reactions that look disproportionate with respect to their visible cause. And you can always put it aside for a while, waiting to come back and dig more when it feels right for you.

I have come to believe that our relationship to money is a gold mine to explore triggers because I have never met anyone who does not display some sort of peculiar behavior when it comes to money—have you? Take for example Catherine, a very healthy acquaintance of mine. When she plans for big parties at home, she can drive eight hours back and forth to Italy, France or Germany and buy the dishes she likes for much less than in Switzerland, where she lives. She is not particularly stingy, she is not stupid, and she doesn't enjoy driving so much that any excuse would get her behind the wheel. So, definitely money is not the problem here. It is something that would deserve a deep dive into her seven whys.

Now, if, like me, you are interested in the role that money plays in the world, you might have read economy books or listened to podcasts that explain how money is just a symbol, albeit a very powerful one. So much so, that our entire society revolves around it. But believe me, if it was not money, that basically has no value in itself, and it was gold, or pigs, or diamonds, or any other commodity that played a similar role in the past, very quickly its symbolic value would step on the head of its intrinsic value and people would be ready and willing to suffer, kill, or die for it. As it actually happened in so many places and times on our planet. Yuval Harari, the well-known historian, rightly says that "money is the most universal and most efficient system of mutual trust ever devised"[15]. I personally suspect this strong relationship between money and a fundamental value like trust to be among the roots of our issues with money. The connection between money and trust is unfortunately neither clear nor obvious to most people. Money can therefore mean different things to different people, and these differences may give rise to disagreement and even conflict. Just think about what can happen in families dealing with inheritance issues.

What I can add, having learned it from my own and others' experience, is that our relationship to money is bound to offer each of us a powerful perspective onto our being, our story and our needs, this because of the unique role that it plays, one way or another, in our lives for economic, social, and personal reasons. If only we manage to deconstruct the maze within which all these things lie. And when we come out of the labyrinth, the prize is personal growth, greater clarity, and enhanced freedom. Because otherwise we may become slaves to money, instead of being served by it.

---

[15] Yuval Noah Harari, *Sapiens: A Brief History of Humankind* (Vintage Publishing, 2015), chap. 10, "The Scent of Money".

This brings to my mind an important milestone in my private life, that occurred when Serge and I chose to give up on more wealth to preserve the family's quality of life. Let me explain. We had just found and decided to buy a new house (actually, the one we have been living in for the past two decades). In principle we had to sell the previous one, which was much smaller and could not comfortably host our family anymore, with the birth of our third child. That meant severing our emotional ties with the house that had been our first property, the first home to our two eldest children, a home that we had considerably embellished over the years. I felt torn inside and would have wished not to sell it, so one night Serge and I sat down and made all the necessary calculations to see whether keeping it and renting it out could be an option, after all. The new house was a huge investment for us; it was much bigger and also needed quite some work to be done. However, as mortgage rates were at their lowest point in decades, we could have stretched ourselves out, applied for a much bigger mortgage, and repaid it over a longer period with the help of the anticipated rent revenue, if we rented the old house out.

The idea of keeping the first house appealed strongly to me. But when I realized that for one or two years we would need to cut all non-essential expenditures, including travel, and that we would also have to deal with tenants, my heart sank in my chest and I started panting. That was the physical reaction to the perspective of having to give up on many pleasant experiences and possibilities, and become landlords instead. A severe attack on our freedom, which had just been increased by the purchase of a bigger house.

I also recalled that, over the previous year or so, I had constantly felt like a prisoner in the first house, feeling a sense of oppression in my chest, because it had not been designed to host a family of five. And now we were looking at the option of feeling even less at ease, with two houses on our back and all this entailed in terms of maintenance, mortgage and tenant vs. landlord issues. It didn't take much time for both Serge and me to grasp that keeping the first house seemed like a great move on paper, as it would have made us wealthier, but actually it would have also stressed us a lot.

We decided not to run that risk and promptly sold the first house.

I have never regretted that choice. It made us less well-off, but we gained in inner peace and did not need to give up on our holiday dreams and other opportunities for fun, gratitude, awe, and discovery.

We also gained time, which is humankind's scarcest resource and has become my favorite commodity. Time. I have always been fascinated by this concept, considering that time is the fourth dimension of our universe. How wondrous! A dimension that manifests and is measured totally differently compared to height, width, and length, the other three dimensions. And time may find itself in a special relationship to money, as people may need lots of time to make up for the lack of money. I lovingly remember my grandmothers, who spent most of their lives as housewives in very disadvantaged socio-economic settings, so much so that they could rarely afford to buy meat or fish for the whole family. To prepare nutritious meals with less expensive staple food like pulses, vegetables, and pasta required them to spend hours sweating in the kitchen, so that humble food could still appeal to their families and nourish them sufficiently.

My relationship with time has evolved as I have stepped up in my career and my salary has increased following each promotion. The result is that today I can, and I am, ready to pay a lot to preserve my time and choose where to invest it. Time is the ultimate enabler, as it comes in unknown and finite quantities to each of us. I have come to the point that I do not hesitate to spend money if this can free precious moments in my day.

In this respect too, my learning curve has been quite steep and has gone through painful milestones that have turned into unforgettable lessons for me. One of them was the "taxi-in-Bangkok experience", as my family refers to it.

It happened in April 2012. We were in Thailand with the kids, and we were very excited at everything we were discovering together: the hustle and bustle of Bangkok, a huge and enthralling metropole, its gorgeous temples, flamboyant parks, and delicious food. It was a dream come true!

One day we decided to visit the Grand Palace, one of the absolute must-see spots in the capital. Our hotel overlooked the Chao Phraya river in the southern part of the city and was situated at a distance of around seven kilometers (four and a half miles) from the centrally located Grand Palace. That day the weather was unsurprisingly tropical, hitting almost 40°C (104°F) with 80% humidity. The sun was peaking in the sky, and no decent public transport was available between the two places. Moreover, we were a family of five, including our three children. Serge set out to negotiate the price with the taxi drivers waiting in front of the hotel.

None of them asked for less than $15USD. I realized that they were asking about 50% more than the normal price. I refused to get into any of those cabs. I believed that they were plotting against us, seeing that we were a big family and reckoning that we would swallow such an unjustified price. I insisted that we should rather start walking, as we would likely find more acceptable taxi pricing a bit further away from the hotel.

My usual trigger caused by the fear of being scammed had been set off. Serge was not pleased and tried to reason with me, but I stubbornly insisted. The problem was that from there on, we did not come across any available taxis. We ended up walking for more than two hours under an unforgiving sun, with the children heavily complaining about the heat and their growing discomfort and Serge refusing to even talk to me until much later in the afternoon.

I don't dare to imagine what you are thinking right now. I definitely felt shame, guilt, and regret already that afternoon, and still for a long time afterward. How could I possibly cause so much suffering to the people I loved most—and to myself—for money? Not to mention the underlying issue of trust. Clearly, all my math missed the critical point: that if we can afford something and spare pain and suffering, we can enjoy our freedom and act compassionately. But I was not free. My trigger had completely blocked out compassion. It had created a narrow tunnel vision in my mind: I could see only my fear of being scammed and react from that emotion. I was neither present nor mindful of the circumstances, and I ended up behaving in a way that could have brought serious consequences for the health of my loved ones.

Since then I have learned to put needs first, and forget about my savvy calculations. I have come to appreciate time more and more. And I feel totally safe when relating to money. Because of my personal history, I know I hardly run the risk of erring on the side of wasting money, so I can feel free to test and try new ways of spending. Today I can even get scammed on the internet without being triggered. I can say it for sure, because it has already happened to me. I can finally take it and accept that scams are a part of life, sometimes unavoidable, but entirely manageable. And I have decided to enjoy more and more of what money can truly offer me. Time for sure, but also opportunities to express my gratitude to people, to welcome more awe and wonder into my life and the lives of the people I love, and to take care of them and of myself in many different ways.

I know I am a work in progress, still getting rid of my limiting beliefs concerning money and what I can allow myself to do with it. But instead of being hard on myself, every time I discover and grab a new opportunity I tell myself, "I am proud of you. I know you are doing your best." Curiosity has become my greatest ally in this process. It gently nudges me into testing new ways to use money and create value, have fun, spur positive emotions, make pleasant experiences happen, and create lasting memories. And I strive to become more generous every day by learning from inspiring examples around me: Serge surprising me with a new taste of chocolate, our children buying a toy for our cat Fuji, my friends sending me good-wish flowers, or my colleagues bringing sweets to the office from their last vacation.

Approaching my triggers and limiting beliefs about money from a place of self-compassion has helped me to unravel my relationship with money and to grow. It is not easy and it is not quick, considering that society generally holds money as the currency of our intrinsic value and one of the main benchmarks of success. It may also be painful, because we rarely relate to money in a neutral way, and the road to a more balanced relationship with money is often scattered with difficult emotions, strong triggers, and unpleasant memories. But when we start questioning unhelpful assumptions about our net worth, we may discover many more creative and fruitful ways to address the money issue. We can get free from excessive dependence and look at money from a mindful vantage point, to discover what it can bring to us in our own unique way because of who we are, instead of putting ourselves in the service of money.

Finally, it seems to me that a more skillful approach to money can only come from our personal quest for wisdom. A good exercise could be to write down all the things that money can't buy and dwell for a while on this list. This is where we will find what we value most, and start inquiring with ourselves why, and what we would be ready to give up to get—or to keep—what is truly valuable. Shall we give it a try?

To summarize and help you practice, through meditation, journaling, or self-reflection, I have listed here the self-inquiry questions underpinning chapter 10:

- What's money got to do with success in my view?
- How would I describe my relationship to money?
- Can I think of a situation that triggered me about money (or anything else) and ask "why?" up to seven times to get to the bottom of it?
- How can I qualify the value of time to me? Any example?
- How can my relationship to money make me grow? Can I recall a situation where this has already happened?
- In my opinion, what are the things that money can't buy? Looking at the list of these things, which ones do I value most? Why? What would I be ready to give up to get—or to keep—those?

And you can add your own self-inquiry questions below:

_____
_____
_____
_____
_____

Finally, I have selected a resource for you that I find very powerful in connection with this chapter, a meditation practice guided by Neelama Eyres during my Applied Compassion Training module on triggers in March 2021: https://www.thevirtualsanctuary.live/spiritual-teachings

For more, don't hesitate to browse through my "Recommended Resources" at the end of the book.

CHAPTER ELEVEN

Getting to Joy

Revival, Greg Porter

Fun is not something I do easily. Due to my "girls-only" style of upbringing, during the first two decades of my life much of the talk was about duty, modesty, good manners, sacrifice, and the like. Fun was frowned upon like a usual suspect: it could only distract a girl, or even steer her away from the duties stemming from her nature. As a baby, toddler, and little girl I had been very playful, funny, curious and always ready to embark on a new adventure, like for example scavenging my parents' bedroom wardrobe in search of forbidden treasures. That obviously came with a cost: shouting, punishment, or even just my parents' disappointed look. Was fun, this fleeting experience that leaves hardly any trace, really worth it? So, as soon as I learned to read and started going to school, I became quieter and quieter, moving my mischievous interactions with real life to the fascinating realm of story-telling and imagination, where fun belonged to me only. I was free to activate it when I wished so, with no fear of consequences.

Joy, on the contrary, came naturally to me. I mean joy as the glow of happiness. No need to invent games or tricks; joy would make me giggle for no reason, light up my face, explode in loud belly laughs. Sometimes secret and understated, other times bursting out like an eruption (I was born under a volcano, remember?), always present in my smile. As a young girl, rare were the days where I would not feel any joy.

Then joy also turned into a mere trickle, until it dried up. My tireless smile turned sad, and I entered a period in my life when I was totally unable to enjoy myself. Sadness had become my real master, and it felt like I was sealed within a pitch black cell.

I was barely seven at that time. My parents still tell me that they could not believe that the playful, curious, creative and ever-smiling child I had always been had morphed into a silent, weepy and inconsolable little girl that would regularly ask them: "What is the purpose of life? Why are we alive? What for?" For the first time the notion of purpose was actually inviting itself into my life, and promptly making a mess of me. My parents could not start to grasp how their little sunshine would make herself miserable by thinking day and night about a question that, in their view, only God was able to answer.

On my side, the very tenuous memories I have of that period revolve around the fact that I had lost both my energy and my enthusiasm for life. As if a life without purpose was not worth the game. Much later did I come to realize that I was experiencing the dark place of despair, a place so many people I know have experienced too.

I distinctly remember how it all started. When I was six, my father, who has always been fond of classical music, convinced me that it would be fabulous if I learned to play piano. He was passionate about music, and piano was his preferred instrument. Truth is, I totally shared his passion for music. For example, I was the sort of child who could spend hours reading, and my pleasure would be enhanced if Beethoven's "Tempest" Sonata was playing in the background. So, his suggestion seemed like an excellent idea to me.

My father wanted of course to get me a very good teacher. We were living in Milan at that time, so somebody recommended a renowned piano teacher to him, one who, among other things, was also the assistant orchestra director at La Scala (surprise, surprise!). It was a Canadian lady whom I believed to be very old because of her gray hair and thick glasses—my educated guess today is that she must have been around 45. I confusedly sensed that her association with the opera house, a place adults always mentioned with respect and reverence, meant that I could not take piano playing lightly. At the same time, the lady, who had two friendly golden cockers, a beautiful house, and a black Steinway grand piano, was so busy that she would regularly cancel or postpone my classes. As a consequence, I visited her (very far-away) place less than once a month and I forgot everything I had learned in between classes. While I loved studying for school, I dreaded the time I had to waste, and take away from studying, writing, and reading, my favorite occupations, to repeat the same stupid musical scales as the month before. I found it so boring and useless!

This unfortunate unraveling of my musical initiation, together with the awareness that my father would feel quite disappointed if I told him how I felt about my piano classes, pushed me into meaninglessness day after day. I was depressed for more than a year. Life seemed to have stopped smiling at me. Experiences that usually would have made me sparkle with anticipation and brim with energy dimmed down to flavorless moments.

I don't recall what finally pushed me out of the black hole, so I have settled for the touch of grace. The fact is that one day I overcame my fear of letting my father down. I spoke up, gently explaining to my parents that I liked studying school subjects much more than music, and that it would certainly be better for me to focus on school only.

Still today, it's hard for me to believe that I managed to articulate such a clear and persuasive argument as a young girl, but my parents confirm that this is what happened. I had been awfully afraid that my father would unleash his anger on me, yet my unbearable sadness made me brave. To my total surprise, he reacted by hugging me and almost apologizing, a gesture that I know has never been easy for him. He admitted that he was light-years from imagining that what he considered so noble and beautiful could make me so miserable. That put an end to my piano lessons (and to my blossoming friendship with the two cute cockers) and little by little brought joy back into my life. I put aside the question that caused my first depressive spell and went back to enjoy life like a carefree little girl.

I reckoned that I had gotten my intake of sadness and despair early in life, and I grew up with the conviction that I had learned the hard way how to avoid the abyss of depression. As if I had been vaccinated against it. Unfortunately, this was not the case. In the early 2000s, I went back to black.

This time the cause didn't have much to do with my family life: I was a happy wife and the proud mother of two little angels. However, that year turned out to be very challenging at work because of another unexpected reorganization, and for a reason that I still cannot grasp my mind started ruminating on a very simple, yet frightening question: why does evil exist? Why do people have to suffer? What for? Another heavy inquiry opening up almost 30 years after my first pit-stop at Depression Land. Clearly, I have a thing for existential problems: first meaning and purpose, then evil and suffering. Serge tried his best to cheer me up, as the loving and supportive partner he has always been, and that certainly helped. But what gave me the grit and the strength to go against the tide of depression were two considerations, one cognitive, the other emotional.

On one side, I started wondering whether the problem was linked to the nature of the question. Instead of (figuratively) banging my head on the wall trying to find an acceptable cause of evil, I could explore the hypothesis that it was possible to ask wrong questions, meaning questions that there is no way we could ever find a logical answer to. I ended up accepting that I had been asking the wrong question all along, because after months and months of inquiring and searching neither had I been able to find any convincing answer, nor did I know of anyone who had. A much more useful question would have been "what can I do in the presence of evil/pain/suffering? How can I respond to that?" I started realizing that, if I tweaked the question appropriately, it became possible to answer it.

At the same time, I decided to bring more warmth and light into my days, beginning with the morning. Without yet knowing anything about our negativity bias[16], I chose to devote some time to look at the sky as soon as I woke up, to awake wonder, positively influence my mood from the start of the day, and try to force more joy into my life.

This creative approach was not the result of savvy teachings or sophisticated therapies. It was based solely on my intuition, activated and spurred by despair. And surprisingly, at least for me, it worked fabulously. It did not take long for me to get out of the depression cave, as I was experiencing every day a stronger sense of agency, positivity, awe, and joy. I did not know at that time that I was practicing letting go of the bad and letting in the good, as Rick Hanson explains in his science-based book *Hardwiring Happiness*[17]. Because neuroscience shows that, if we fill our inner space with negative feelings and thoughts, hardly any room is left for the positive sides of life. This happens not because we are stupid or unworthy, but because keeping on our guard to spot threat has helped the human species to survive, thereby allowing our negativity bias to develop. We all do this, even though today rare are the situations when a tiger can jump out of a bush and devour us. However, as research shows,

---

[16] https://greatergood.berkeley.edu/article/item/how_to_overcome_your_brains_fixation_on_bad_things.

[17] Rick Hanson, *Hardwiring Happiness: The New Brain Science of Contentment, Calm, and Confidence* (Harmony Books, 2013).

neuroplasticity enables us to rewire our brain. In other words, we can reformat our mind, so to speak, to counter our negativity bias if we decide to pay more attention to what is good in our life. The result being that, when we practice letting go of the bad, we actually make space inside, and if we replace the negative (memories, feelings, experiences) with more positive elements we shift our balance towards happiness. By practicing letting go and letting in we change and become more attentive to the positive aspects of life, more confident, secure, and happy.

Well before diving into my compassion studies, neuroplasticity was already making miracles in my life with the help of the Fantastic Four, as I like to call the qualities that bring more happiness into our life when we choose to cultivate them: self-compassion, awe, gratitude, and joy. I have already spoken much about self-compassion and how it has changed my life. Let me now turn to the other members of the quartet.

Awe, in particular, deserves a medal for pulling me out of the black hole I was in at the dawn of the new millennium. Simply reconnecting with my innate ability to marvel at the break of day was enough to make space quickly for positive emotions in my heart, leaving my gloomy cogitations in the background. Talking of this, I distinctly remember that, when I was a child in Milan, I used to spend hours watching the rain from my window, in awe. And you, my dear reader, have you ever realized how sophisticated the dance of rain can be? How the wind can make it swirl around, and then let it drop vertically like tiny icicles? And how the lines it leaves on the window glass can be elaborate, and subtly fascinating? As adults, we rarely talk about the beauty of rain, but if we visit our child's heart even for a brief moment, I bet we can feel awe again for rain and for a host of forgotten, humble wonders. Would you like to try? And how does it feel in your body?

Gratitude is another incredible resource that we all have in abundance—once we realize it. It is one of the forces that connects us to the people we interact with, at least potentially. Not convinced? Then bear with me, and just imagine forming a circle with those who are present in your life. Now you are playing a game together. The rules are simple. A member of the circle holds a ball, and they have to throw the ball to another person in the circle. The person who receives it has to express gratitude to that person, giving a specific reason. Then the receiver has to throw the ball to another person, who also expresses gratitude to the sender, and the game goes on. The rule is that the game stops only when everybody has given and received gratitude. I am ready to bet you are already noticing reasons for being grateful, even very simple ones you had rarely given thought to.

Years ago, I played this game with my entire team. It was a glorious day in June in the Belgian countryside, where we were enjoying a beautiful team building experience outside the conference center of a light-filled hotel, just after the end of the pandemic. Our facilitator had decided to place this special ball game at the very end of the team building. Everybody was having fun, and saying very nice things about those who had thrown the ball to them. When my turn arrived to throw the ball, I threw it to one of my assistants, an endearing young man who was generally quite shy. I was moved to my core when he said to me, loud and clear, "I want to thank you because you have made me feel worthy and appreciated since the first day we met. Thank you for all the trust you have placed in me. I'll continue doing my best not to disappoint you."

I did not know much then about gratitude from a scientific point of view, but I can still feel the emotions that flowed from my assistant's expression of thanks toward me. I felt a surge of surprise in my body; I imagine that I even blushed for a couple of seconds. Then I felt my heart warming up, and a sensation of ease rippled out from my chest to the rest of the body. I briefly thanked him, and then I noticed that his words kept on emerging several times inside me, like waves gently crashing on the beach, each of them bringing along a feeling of satisfaction and joy. At the same time, I could also feel some embarrassment. But this unpleasant, diffuse sensation decreased little by little, to make space for full acceptance of my assistant's expression of gratitude.

I was curious to understand more about the surge of embarrassment in my body. Could it be that it was there to express that accepting his thanks pointed to a vulnerability of mine? Of course it did, in some way. Because if we had it all, if we were always in control and on top of things, if we did not need anyone or anything, then there would be no reason to be thankful or to graciously accept others' gratitude for us. In that moment, I could experience gratitude as a shining manifestation of our common humanity.

Deflecting or dodging his gratitude would have been my first instinct. But why should I refuse it? He was absolutely right. I had believed in him and in his professional skills from the very beginning, even though I knew he still needed to learn many things to become an outstanding assistant.

But he was a clever and hard-working guy; he had lots of goodwill and a good heart. So, I had taken a bet on him and offered him a temporary contract, firmly believing that I could help him grow as an assistant. And this is exactly how the story developed: today he is a permanent official, leading by example and appreciated for his results, professionalism, and loyalty to the institution.

What I had never considered was that he might realize what led me to pick him, among many other candidates. I was simply unaware of how my decision had landed with him. That meant that I was not clear about my impact on others, and I was not focusing enough on my power of agency. This, in turn, was limiting my freedom to deploy my full potential for goodness. I realized in that moment that actually I could bring much more to everybody around me if I became aware of who I was and what I was capable of. Unbelievable how a simple gesture of gratitude could unveil something crucial that I had not understood about myself until then!

I suddenly realized that for him, and possibly others, I had become a role model. Someone to emulate because we admire them for their qualities. And that reminded me of my own role models. Those who had acted toward me the way I had unconsciously acted toward him. In a sense, history was repeating itself. For example, you may remember Zelia, my inspiring school teacher between first and fourth grade. She had definitely seen, accepted, valued, and loved me for who I was, with my thick glasses, my round shape and all. She had not only allowed me to grow under her loving and gentle lead, but she had gone the extra mile and invited me to do special things, like being the buddy of one of my schoolmates with a mental disability, or helping her to assess new geography and history books for third-grade pupils. I remember the joy, gratitude and pride I could feel in my little heart whenever I met her loving gaze, a privilege I had every day for over three years. And I realize today that her deep affection and keen support helped me build the resilience and inner strength that enabled me to survive bullying and harassment. She was my own David Richo, the reputed academic and psychotherapist who identified what he calls the 5 As of love: Attention, Acceptance, Appreciation, Affection, and Allowing[18]. My teacher saw, welcomed, valued, and loved me for who I was, and gave me space, trusting that I could become even more of who I was. I am forever grateful to her for having seen my light and having cultivated my intellectual and human qualities with love and kindness, as only great educators can do.

I have been lucky enough to meet and learn from other wonderful people who also became role models for me. Please meet Lina, my math teacher in lower secondary school. She was my mother's age and, by total coincidence, lived in the same apartment block that we had moved into on coming back from Milan—I could actually see and greet her from my kitchen balcony! She was a fiery lady with a mane of shiny, wavy brown hair whom I immediately admired for her character, intelligence, and beauty. Little did I know then of her inner battles and self-doubt, let alone that I triggered her due to my excellent results in mathematics. Surprising for a math teacher, right? Later, she opened up and revealed to me that

---

[18] David Richo, *How to Be an Adult in Relationships: The Five Keys to Mindful Loving* (Shambhala Publications, 2021).

her true passion was actually biology. She had studied life sciences at university, but in order to get a job at our secondary school she had been obliged to teach mainly math, a subject that she deeply disliked and felt very uncomfortable with. From this she developed what today would be called a huge imposter syndrome that haunted her for many years.

Our first contact as teacher and pupil was far from ideal. It happened at the beginning of my first secondary school year. She was quizzing the class on the properties of division. Everybody kept silent, so she repeated the explanations, and then asked again. I was extremely shy, still I forced myself to put my hand up—the only pupil daring to do so. She doubted that her teachings had been clear, so she asked me to repeat the properties out loud, which I did faultlessly. As she told me later, from that first direct encounter she deducted that I spent all my free time studying and developed a certain contempt for me. Today we would say that she did not like nerds. However, that misunderstanding did not last long. November came, and so did our first class trip. She was among the accompanying teachers. During the hours spent on the road, to fight boredom we started singing songs from popular Japanese cartoon series for kids, like *UFO Robot Grendizer* or *Godzilla*. She noticed that I sang every song enthusiastically, without skipping a single lyric. She realized that her harsh judgment on me was unfounded and felt obliged to make amends.

I was extremely surprised the day she approached me at the end of a math class and invited me over to her place "to get to know each other better, as we are close neighbors." I felt honored and excited, and I ran home fueled by joy. I seem to remember that I even prepared a cake together with my mom to thank my teacher for her gesture. It was then that she confessed to me how she had perceived me first, and how she had come to understand that her hasty judgment was totally wrong. I realize now that her brave and humble admission was likely one of the first seeds that led me to stop minding apologizing.

The conversation that followed was sparkling and covered a lot of grounds. She explained her love for science. I described how much I loved math. Since that moment we developed a beautiful teacher-student relationship that was steeped in humility and respect. Two years later, when she was facing health challenges, she even asked whether I could assist her in correcting my schoolmates' math homework. I accepted with joy: her recognition meant the world to me. Lina was a "coping role model", as Amy Edmondson[19], the scholar who identified the importance of psychological safety at work, would put it: an inspiring figure that handles failure through the acceptance of vulnerability and overcomes it by being self-compassionate. Today I know that Lina was a compassionate leader who embraced authenticity, resilience, and humility in a way I had never witnessed before or after. Until I met my most inspiring boss at work, Sebastian.

Funnily enough, my début as a manager under his authority was at least as stormy as my first contact with Lina. The problem was that I had been appointed by Daniel, a boss with whom I got on really well. But I reported directly to Sebastian, and the two men could not have been more apart. So, of course, the first months were rocky for me, as I had to navigate whatever was happening above my head while keeping up a flawless

---

[19] For more information on Amy Edmonson's work and publications, you can go to https://amycedmondson.com/books/.

behavior toward both. I wanted each of them to trust me fully. It was of course easier with my big boss. He knew that I was totally loyal to him from the start, among other things because I owed him my promotion. For Sebastian it was altogether different, as he did not have a choice and could naturally doubt my loyalty toward him. If I wanted to avoid tension at work, I needed to earn his trust.

And I did, always going first to him on any issue and refraining from using my special access to the big boss to get decisions or resources more quickly. At the beginning, my behavior was merely a skillful strategy, but it swiftly evolved into genuine appreciation for my line manager. I became aware that I could learn a lot, as a professional and as a human being, from his vast experience and wisdom. He was almost 20 years older than me and his life journey had been amazing. For starters, his socio-economic background was extremely modest, similar to my grandparents'. I still remember a conversation with him while we were walking across one of the historical neighborhoods of Madrid, going from our hotel to a conference where we featured among the speakers. Suddenly he told me that he had lived in that area and he referred to his childhood, spent in a tiny place where everybody was sleeping in the same room. He told me how going to university had been an extraordinary undertaking for somebody as poor as him. He also told me of the courage he had needed to decide to move to Germany with his wife and little daughter, because he hardly spoke German and had never lived outside Spain. He learned the language, and later he even enrolled in a recruitment competition for linguists organized just before Spain joined the European Union. He described how incredulous he was when he learned that he had passed it. He felt as if an impossible dream had come true, for someone like him who was born and raised during Franco's dictatorship. Sebastian was not known for being talkative. But somehow, that day and during the few years that we worked together before he retired, he came to recognize me as akin to him. I received his friendship as a precious gift and felt really sad when he left for Spain after three decades of European public service.

When I look at my amazing role models, I realize that what they modeled for me were behaviors grounded in the values that have always been dear to my heart. When I say "values", I mean the qualities that I wish to see in my life. Love and compassion in the first place, of course; but also humility, freedom, wisdom, and justice. What about you?

Values fuel our motivation, shape our action, shine through our purpose. They dress happiness in the unique way and style that corresponds to us. And joy gives voice and color to our happiness. Let's just take a moment to reconnect with the deepest experiences of joy in our life. Here are the experiences that top my list:

- The day I got married: that made my lifelong love dream come true;
- The days I gave birth to my children: each of them brought awe, humility, and another version of unconditional love into my life;
- The day I was offered a lifetime job as a European civil servant: that came with purpose, safety, financial security, and growth perspectives;
- The day I received the product safety award: that made me feel appreciated and recognized as a global leader in my professional area.

But what has consistently surprised me is that I am able to find joy almost in every moment of my life if I intentionally look for it. Because I do believe, in the words of Brother Steindl-Rast[20], a respected scholar active in the field of interreligious dialogue, that "joy is the happiness that does not depend on what happens. It is the grateful response to the opportunity that life offers you at this moment." OK, that can be hard. And I recognize that this seemingly simple quote weighs tons in terms of wisdom, awareness, equanimity, surrender, freedom, love, and life experience. So, let's take a deep breath and pause for a moment here.

For sure, it is extremely challenging to find a grateful response in painful moments, for example when we lose someone we love, or our job, or when we discover that we have a serious health condition. I would certainly not suggest that you start by facing that with gratitude as a first step, unless you happen to be a saint or an especially awakened being. Just to put things into perspective, I can assure you that many are the situations where joy does not immediately emerge from my heart. Yet, I have discovered that joy lingers in us even in the most difficult moments. When those moments happen, we certainly need plenty of self-compassion first to soothe our suffering. Then it is possible to reignite the joy—sometimes just by feeling grateful for our beating heart, or our breath. I have experienced that, and I am sure you can too, as a fellow human being. Would you like to test it with something that is moderately annoying, just to practice opening your heart space to joy? Later on, you may want to try the same strategy with something a bit more challenging, and see how it goes. I try to practice opening up to joy often, whenever I think of

---

[20] Brother Steindl-Rast cited in Dalai Lama & Tutu, *The Book of Joy*.

it, indeed. And you know what? Knowing that you may try it too is now filling me with joy. And hope: that one day we may all experience the kind of joy that does not depend on what happens, as Brother Steindl-Rast wisely said. I would call that true happiness. What about you?

To summarize and help you practice, through meditation, journaling, or self-reflection, I have listed here the self-inquiry questions underpinning chapter 11:

- Is having fun important to me? And why?
- What does joy mean to me? Can I recall an experience that brought deep joy to me?
- When I explore the reasons why I live, what emerges from inside?
- What can I do in the presence of evil/pain/suffering? How can I respond to that?
- Can I feel awe again for forgotten, humble wonders? Watching the dance of the rain, for example? And how does it feel in my body?
- What are my values, the fundamental qualities I want to see in my life?
- Can I list the moments I felt deepest joy in my entire life?
- Can I recall an experience in my life where I could connect with joy even if I was suffering? How does my body experience this?
- What would I call true happiness?

And you can add your own self-inquiry questions below:

_____

_____

_____

_____

Finally, I have selected a resource for you that I find very powerful in connection with this chapter, a project supported by UC Berkeley's Greater Good Science Center called "The Big Joy": https://ggia.berkeley.edu/bigjoy

For more, don't hesitate to browse through my "Recommended Resources" at the end of the book.

CHAPTER TWELVE

Aligning with Purpose through Compassion

Grateful, Rita Ora

I can feel terribly angry. Still today, many of my triggers activate anger or ire, rumbling like a volcano in my guts. This does not mean I cannot feel sad, or fearful, or anxious. I bet you still remember my school trauma from being bullied, that consistently sent me into freeze mode in the face of violence. But my personal history and some situations buried since my childhood have connected me strongly with the fight reaction to a threat, and tap into the energy of ire. I know many people whose triggers involve other emotions, different because they are expressions of different roots. In my case, I can allow myself to feel the burning explosion of anger in my chest because I have learned that this will decrease its intensity.

I never yelled at my colleagues, apart from one or two occasions—and that happened among peers. I have never considered it acceptable to exert authoritarian power on colleagues who reported to me, as this kind of relationship is asymmetrical and they would generally not feel free to stand up to me, their boss. However, at times I could allow myself to raise my voice at my children, because I felt entitled to do so by motherhood. As if Mama Bear could afford to scare her cubs to shield them from a threat (as perceived by her). I don't feel proud when I admit that it took me a long time to become aware of my lack of humility as a mother. But there was a silver lining in that painful moment of growth: I knew that from then on, I could become not only a better mother, but also a much better person.

Of course, we all want to become a better version of ourselves. However, we all have different ways to express this. For example, at some point Serge told me something that left me puzzled. That day he held me in a long, loving look and said, "Now you are in your place."

"I beg to differ," I replied, after a pause.

"Sorry, what do you mean?"

I could read confusion and a tad of disappointment in his eyes. As if he felt that I was not welcoming something coming from him that was more than a simple compliment. I knew he was convinced that my key existential question was about finding the right place. Saying that I was in my place to him meant that I had become fully myself, grounded in my being. So, I took a deep breath and clarified, "I know you mean well. It's just that I would not express it that way. For me, it's not a question of place. I have always felt steeped in myself, grounded in unconditional love. My homeland is inside me."

"You know I am not referring to a physical place," he gently protested.

"Exactly. That's why what really speaks to me is alignment. Alignment with my purpose."

We were actually saying the same thing, I realized. Only the metaphors differed, for reasons linked to our past and our education, our experiences, and our needs. So, what he called "the right place" meant for me "alignment with purpose". And maybe you would call it something else.

In my heart, I wish this alignment to everybody, in every aspect of life. For me, this includes the workplace I dream of. A place where everybody can feel safe, connected to their purpose, respected, trusted, valued, and appreciated for who they are and what they bring to the world as professionals. Of course, I know this is often not what we find, and please do not count me among those who consider that the only good worker is one who really loves their job[21], because that depends on so many factors that it would be unfair, in my opinion, to place this heavy expectation on the shoulders of anyone. Moreover, our fundamental needs and wish to provide for our loved ones may oblige us to accept jobs that are far from ideal for us. However, all those who practice a professional activity may influence their workplace and can potentially make a difference. And of course, the more responsibility your job entails, the more you can attract, hire, and motivate co-workers who have the right profile. This may end

---

[21] You may want to have a look at this interesting analysis of how loving our jobs is evolving into a moral obligation : https://www.workties.org/post/the-moralization-of-intrinsic-motivation-how-loving-work-became-a-moral-imperative.

up creating the virtuous circle that will, little by little, enable everybody in the team to experience the alignment of their job with their life purpose, joyful connection with colleagues, the exciting perspective of contributing to the greater good, and the learning opportunities that will surely emerge: nobody knows everything and we can always learn from obstacles and setbacks.

And yet, I realize that I am not writing only with respect to the workplace. Whatever I have experienced as a consequence of my journey toward compassion at work has abundantly rippled out to every other aspect of my existence. Over the course of my life I have understood the meaning of alignment as bringing my purpose in line with how I show up in every aspect of life and with what I pursue. Bringing people together, bridging divides, and finding our common root, ground, needs, and responses has become my compass.

Needless to say, every life, every purpose is unique. I don't have any secret recipe for wisdom or shortcut to happiness. However I am fully convinced that the way to get there for everyone is to increase self-awareness and grow into who we are.

My personal journey has unlocked self-compassion. Thanks to it, I have become fully aware that there is a gift in every sorrow, if our hearts are open enough to welcome it. It's far from easy, and the deeper the hurt, the more wisdom—and time—required to discover the gift it brings. The foundations of compassion, mindfulness, common humanity, and humility are our best allies in this. In particular, mindfulness frees our capacity to recognize the common human fabric of everything around us, and see through the lens of humility that we belong to humankind. Humility was possibly the most precious treasure hidden in my Stanford classes: I was familiar with the concept of not feeling fundamentally more or better than others, but I had never grasped the other, liberating face of humility, reminding us that neither are we beneath anyone. This insight invites us to pursue a point of balance that is continuously shifting, due to our changing circumstances and the way we adapt to them. It also constantly reminds us that we are and remain nothing less and nothing more than everybody else, no matter what happens.

What does this entail in terms of power of agency? For example, when we see the ocean of suffering that sends its waves crashing all over the world? Countless are the situations where I have experienced a sense of impotence and helplessness—just like you, dear reader, I'm ready to bet. Against this background, humility has taught me that we can do no more and no less than what is contained in our sphere of action and influence. So, I cannot do much more than praying to stop the wars devastating several countries right now as I am finishing this book. But I can comfort my daughter when she loses a dear friend, and I can lighten the tasks of a colleague who is feeling overwhelmed.

This gave me wings: appreciating that our agency and our responsibility fully and only cover what is in our power to influence or change. So much so that compassion and love dawned on me as the full version of my life purpose during my studies in applied compassion, imprinting them on my being.

My teachers at Stanford call this phenomenon "embodiment". At the beginning of the program, they had explained that if we not only studied the components of compassion, but also practiced them regularly, we would get to feel compassion and experience it directly, without having to go through thoughts. I felt quite skeptical at first about this promised development, because I doubted that I could skip the thinking part in anything I did. But here I am, self-confessed culprit of hasty judgments. The embodiment of compassion happened to me quite fast, taking me by surprise. Those who share my everyday life—my family, friends, and colleagues—were the first to notice. They perceived a new kind of glow from me. I appeared to be much calmer. I stopped multitasking. I became less stressed and more intentional in my actions.

Truth is, I was already scoring quite high on the happiness index before my Applied Compassion Training studies. The embodiment of compassion (which happened to many ACT students, just to confirm that it was a widespread consequence of both studying and practicing compassion) brought me to the next compassionate level, and completely unlocked my courage in the area of compassion. For starters, when Helen asked me to offer monthly Compassion Breaks to our colleagues in June 2021, well before my ACT graduation, instead of crumbling beneath the weight of imposter syndrome, I boldly accepted. Until that moment I had never guided a meditation for others, let alone in English, my third language. My heart was trembling, and I was telling myself that I would fail miserably; still, I agreed. I designed and delivered the sessions, and many colleagues gave me very positive feedback.

My department also asked me to offer our staff something about compassion, considering the widespread suffering and the social distancing brought about by the pandemic. When I did so for the first time, in the beginning of July 2021, nobody joined my online session. I was not pleased, of course; and I wondered whether I could ever become a conduit of compassion in my own workplace. Notwithstanding my doubts and worries, I bet on the reasonable explanation that internal communication about the session had been minimal and was hidden somewhere in our vast corporate website. So, I decided to give compassion a second chance two months later, and since then many colleagues from different departments have regularly come to my sessions and shown deep appreciation for them.

My way of being a spouse, a mother, and a daughter was evolving too. I became much more patient, understanding, and constructive where before I might have gone down the path of irritation, stubbornness, and anger.

※ ※ ※

At work, as you may remember, I had grown more and more into compassionate leadership. I had always striven to be good to my colleagues, trying to make their lives as easy as possible so that they could give their utmost. However, I was often unsure on how to address conflict properly, and whether I could really help if they had issues at home. With the courage of compassion came clarity of purpose, and my professional and human compasses ended up aligning: now I know deep down in my heart that whatever I do to decrease my colleagues' suffering, be it at work or at home, helps them to be happier and perform at higher levels and have greater policy impact. In the last few years my colleagues and I had the beautiful but daunting task of conceiving, writing, and negotiating the new European law on general product safety. Thanks to compassion, my team flourished more than ever, becoming a real community of hearts and values, a safe and supportive haven for all. In spite of the pandemic, scarcity of resources, and very strong corporate pressure, since 2021 nobody in my team has had a burnout: I take this as an indicator that working relationships among us have been nurtured by compassion.

But the miracle of compassion did not stop there. Thanks to a number of colleagues active in the area of mindfulness and compassion in my organization, to the moral and scientific support of my Stanford mentors and Center for Compassionate Leadership (CFCL) teachers, and to the warm embrace of the growing global community of Compassion Ambassadors, I became bolder in designing new compassion-related activities and offering them at work.

To be honest, back in 2021, while I was studying at Stanford, I had hoped for an immediate compassionate transformation of our corporate culture from the top. But my attempt to reach out to the Commission's human resources top management and get their buy-in on an internal strategy for compassion was naively ambitious and came too early in the process. However, I did not give up because of that failure. I was brimming with new ideas and projects (including this book), which gave me the energy and strength to go back to a more humble approach and persevere on the path of compassion.

I decided to turn my strategy on its head. Instead of targeting top managers, whenever a request concerning compassion was addressed to me, no matter by whom, I would respond positively. I started telling everybody that I would never say no to compassion (do you remember the answer of 100-year-old Pinuccia to my third question in the prologue?), and the requests flocked in. The extra energy and time required to prepare for, deliver and follow up on these sessions came on top of my exciting yet very demanding managerial duties. As well as two regular monthly webinars on topics linked to compassion, one for my department, the other open to all the staff of the European Union, I started giving a double session on compassionate leadership (my certification Capstone project for Stanford) to the young talents of the European Network for Women in Leadership (WIL), a non-profit organization I serve as Secretary-General, and to the female aspiring managers of the Commission. I also started to be invited to all sorts of online and onsite conferences, events, away-days and team-building activities, to speak and give examples of compassion in the workplace, to guide meditations on compassion and self-compassion, and to lead sessions on compassionate leadership.

On top of these activities, many colleagues reach out to me for individual chats, where I simply offer to listen to them with an open and compassionate heart. I find this humbling, heartwarming, and exhilarating. I realize that the ripples of unconditional love that started in my family, both the one I was born into and the one I created with Serge and our children, are widening to embrace more and more people, who happen to be my colleagues but could be anybody on Earth.

Nevertheless, my focus since I started my compassion journey has been on my colleagues in the European institutions. Why so, you may wonder? After all, everybody deserves compassion! That's true. It is also true that another of my life threads leading to who I am today is the European project: the compassionate vision of a continent where peace becomes a defining trait against the backdrop of centuries of ruthless, horrifying wars. Where what we foster together are the values of democracy, equality, justice, fairness, and ultimately the well-being of people[22]. The European Union has a historic mission enshrined in its founding Treaties: to nurture peace and to uphold fundamental rights and humanistic values for the continent. A vision which is being developed, implemented, and built upon day after day, not only for the sake of those who live in Europe, but as a historic experiment that, if successful, can inspire other parts of the world. For this reason, I passionately believe that for the European Commission to get it right as an organization is fundamental not only for Europe, but for humankind. Because if we Europeans, who have spent centuries trying to annihilate each other, can do it, everybody on Earth can do it too. I am a total believer in the value of this endeavor for the whole of humanity.

This precious dream has appealed to me since I was 11. It guided my choice of studies, enabled me to grow into different roles and functions at the European Commission and is now offering a natural outlet to my compassion calling. Because people are always the ultimate asset in any endeavor, and considering the challenging times humankind is currently striving through, I am more convinced than ever that compassion is key to preserve the European dream—for the sake of all human beings.

So, all the major threads of my life have been woven together by compassion and now hold my life purpose: manifesting unconditional love

---

[22] Art. 3.1 of the Treaty on European Union: The Union's aim is to promote peace, its values and the well-being of its peoples. (https://eur-lex.europa.eu/resource.html?uri=cellar:2bf140bf-a3f8-4ab2-b506-fd71826e6da6.0023.02/DOC_1&format=PDF).

and growing compassion together for the greater good. My yearning for success is still present, as lively and strong as ever. What has changed for me over the decades is its meaning.

The question that started that process was: what if success depended on how I look at the world, and not on how the world looks at me? This question and the ensuing reflection paved the way to my shifting from a pre-determined concept of success, which dictated how I should be, act and look as a woman and as a professional, and trusted that external recognition was its measure, to the realization that success is no one-size-fits-all. But then, what could success really mean to me? The epiphany that equals success with being myself started with the deepening of my self-awareness and the decision to live from my core. The courses I followed on compassion cultivation, applied compassion, and compassionate leadership taught me that true and lasting success cannot come from outside. It is built from inside and expressed (more than measured) by our authenticity, in other words by the alignment between our purpose and how we show up in the world. Which is revealed by the degree to which we feel joyful, in the sense that we love and feel loved, we find meaning in life, and we know that we belong. All things that may still be true even in the midst of excruciating experiences. Because once we choose to be true to ourselves, and we make a priority of becoming more so every day, we are as perfect as we are meant to be. And nobody can take that away from us.

Difficult to believe? Well, if aging takes its toll on your memory, you'll quickly realize that no amount of pretending that you do remember will save your face in front of your colleagues. Of course, you can choose to cling to your old self and refuse to accept this unwelcome change. This will not make you a better leader nor entail more compassion for yourself or the others, and will most probably become an obstacle on your path toward being your true self. If, on the contrary, you accept to let go and not only admit to your new reality, but even embrace it and ask your colleagues' support when you don't remember a detail or a date, you will experience a sense of liberation and of gratitude for the help they are offering you. You will be more authentic and your colleagues will perceive you as courageous, while feeling a self-worth boost because they are allowed to help their boss and are thanked for doing so.

Moreover, even when you are in deep suffering, for example because a loved one is seriously ill, you will still be able to hold both the love for that person and the sadness for their suffering or the fear of losing them. This happens because you know and feel that nobody can take away from you the essence of the loving relationship you have experienced with that person.

Of course, sometimes we happen to be granted those awards that mean success in the public eye. Here too, the real question is what they mean to us. A couple of years ago I had the opportunity to delve into deep self-inquiry when the very colleague who won the race for senior manager of my department asked me whether I would accept to become her deputy. On the one hand, I could have reacted badly, because after having been ingloriously kicked out of the race, I now had the offer of being the official "shadow" of my new boss. On the other hand, the offer still represented an unexpected accolade. And if I gave it a generous interpretation, as my Stanford teacher Monica Worline tirelessly recommends, it could mean that my new boss wanted to establish and nurture a constructive working relationship with me. So, what I did was to put everything in context and reflect on the only relevant question from the point of view of "success" as I had come to conceive it: could I lead even more people than before with love and serve with compassion in this new, additional role? Clearly, this would depend on the quality of my relationship with her and the type of tasks that she would entrust to me. I had little doubt as to the quality of our relationship, as she had made the offer with respect, kindness, and enthusiasm. I was also ready to believe that in my new role I could positively influence more colleagues across the department. So, I took the risk and accepted.

I have not regretted it since; I see that I can indeed do good to more people than before. Remembering my first year in cabinets, this is probably what Louis Michel, my then Commissioner, meant when he prophetically told me that I would go far because I was kind. I understand now that for me "going far" equals success in the sense of being who I really am. I am kind by nature, but what I did in that situation was to rescue a colleague who was being unfairly treated. So, even though I was not aware of that back then, my intervention was coming from a place of compassion—fierce compassion, as Kristin Neff defines those acts of compassion that involve speaking up against unfairness or injustice. And Louis Michel saw it and likely used the word "kindness" in the sense of compassion.

And yet, I have discovered that compassion can be not only fierce, but even revolutionary. Indeed, it transforms the way people see themselves. It can lead them to change the world little by little because they have authentically become who they are by accepting their suffering and stopping pretending they can be perfect, in the sense of mimicking a non-existing ideal self—or somebody else. And it is contagious, because once somebody expresses love and compassion, not only will they feel freer to manifest it more often and more boldly, but people around them will be attracted to the wholeness and happiness that shine through them and will want some of this for themselves.

For example, my heart brims with joy when I think of one of my colleagues whom you may remember, Angela. Over a number of years her personal development path has brought her from being on the verge of burnout to cultivating mindfulness and compassion in her life, generously sharing her knowledge and practice with colleagues, and finally growing into a committed compassionate leader. Can you spot anyone who has had a similar trajectory among the people whose paths you have crossed? And if you have difficulties in finding someone around you who has embodied their authentic being, just think about Nelson Mandela, Gandhi, or Martin Luther King: still today, through old footage, television programs and radio recordings, we feel the authenticity of their words and are attracted by the compassion that shines through their being. Of course, they were not perfect—who is? But for sure they were aligned with their purpose and went very far in expressing love, fierce compassion, forgiveness, and faith in common humanity, thus inspiring many other people to act together and leave a lasting, positive impact on the world.

Let me now make a bold statement: there is maybe a way we can reconcile perfection and being our true self. If we look at perfection as a continuous process that enables us to become every day more ourselves, we can conceive being perfect insofar we embody our special, unique way of being, born of unconditional love. This process is perfect in the sense that none other could replace it. This perspective changes the concept of perfection into something very different from what we are accustomed to. It cracks the notion of perfection open to reveal its dynamic and boundless nature. Can you close your eyes and feel it in your bones?

And, yet, I am not giving you a recipe for happiness. I don't think anyone can, for the good reason that we are, all of us, the cooks of our own life. Like Maya Angelou, I believe that a bird doesn't sing because it's giving an answer. It sings because it has a song. What I hope I have been able to make you curious about, along the meandering unfolding of my life, is your own song. This is in my view the pure essence of success: becoming your authentic self and manifesting your life purpose with compassion.

You may wonder at this point how we can measure this kind of success, which doesn't necessarily come with fame, wealth or formal power. I find the answer given by Bob Chapman, CEO of the manufacturing company Barry-Wehmiller, very inspiring: by the way we touch the lives of people. Starting by our own life, may I add.

In conclusion, my invitation to you, dear reader, is to pause and listen to your inner wisdom. I personally do it through meditation, studying, walking in nature, and journaling, but many other avenues—nature, arts, dance, music, cooking, and more—are available, and you will find yours if you follow your preferences, ask yourself powerful questions, and trust what your heart tells you. What counts is that you feel safe and grounded in any circumstance. From that place of safety, you can explore, refine, and express your life purpose: the good you can bring to the world in your own, unique way. I am ready to bet it will be an expression of love. And compassion, which is love in the presence of suffering, will help you develop care, hope and gratitude for yourself and those around you.

Giving an opening to compassion has transformed my life from the inside out, and it has made me happier than ever, even in the midst of deep suffering. I wish that you may experience this special sort of happiness too, in your own way. And that you may find, rediscover, and reinvent, day after day, how to embody your unique purpose and light. Because, as Rumi, the 13th-century poet and Sufi mystic, wrote, "You are not a drop in the ocean. You are the entire ocean in a drop."

To summarize and help you practice, through meditation, journaling, or self-reflection, I have listed here the self-inquiry questions underpinning chapter 12:

- What does success really mean to me? Can I think of a situation where I felt successful? What does it feel like?

- What is a powerful question that can help me listen to my inner wisdom? For example, what matters really to me?

- What does perfection mean to me? Can I remember a specific experience that enabled me to feel perfection in my life?

- Can I relate to anybody who has walked the path of compassionate leadership among the people I have met in life?

- What is my life purpose—or my song, as Maya Angelou would put it?

- If I tell myself "You are not a drop in the ocean, you are the entire ocean in a drop" and listen to my heart, what feelings come up for me?

- Can I think of a quote, a verse, a sentence, or a rhyme that helps me advance on my growth path?

And you can add your own self-inquiry questions below:

_____

_____

_____

_____

Finally, I have selected a resource for you that I find very powerful in connection with this chapter, a video of Thich Nhat Hanh titled "What do you really want?":

https://www.youtube.com/watch?v=uTRX3pbkVdo

For more, don't hesitate to browse through my "Recommended Resources" at the end of the book.

Did You Say "Conclusion"?

Ode to Joy, Symphony n. 9, Ludwig van Beethoven

Conclusions are daunting for me, as they seem to suggest that something—a topic, a conversation, a reflection—can be closed, or even archived, forever. It is true that I have been reflecting, scribbling, re-writing, re-reading, getting feedback from family, friends, and colleagues, modifying, moving around, twisting and tweaking my words, sentences, chapters, and pictures for more than three years before getting to the last dot. And I cannot deny that this is coming with relief, respite, solace, and joy. At the same time, we all probably agree that becoming more and more who we are is a never-ending story. So, my dear reader, let me propose a different way to conclude (while waiting for another book to follow) by handing the temporary conclusion over to you.

Don't tell me you are surprised! Who better than you could find your perfect way to draw the curtain on this endeavor of mine? Just write (or draw/paint/picture) it in the box below, and if you feel like sharing it with me on LinkedIn (https://www.linkedin.com/in/pinuccia-contino/), please do. I look forward to hearing from you, and learning about what my personal journey to redefine success through purpose, authenticity, and compassion has brought to you.

A big "thank you!" from the bottom of my heart—and see you soon, online or in person!

My own conclusion of the book:

Acknowledgements (my way)

Oh my goodness, whom should I start with? And from when? Because there is nothing less lonely to me than writing a book: no way I could have written even a single word without all the people who have come before me, those who have brought me to life (*grazie, mamma e papà!*), those who have loved me, with whom I have interacted all along my life, those I love, and those I cross on my path.

However, to avoid doubling the number of pages, I will only single out those without whom this book would not be the same.

My wholehearted gratitude goes to:

- Coach Number One, also known as Serge, the man I love: without you, I would not be who I am, and you, dear reader, would be reading another book.
- My beloved family: without you, another person would have written the book.
- Alena: without you, this book would not exist.

- Jim, my incomparable mentor, friend, and editor: without you, this book would not have grown from a first awkward draft into a fully-fledged book project.
- Éamon, my amazing beta reader: without you and your helpful suggestions, this book would not have found its unique voice.
- Robert Cusick, Neelama Eyres, Laura Berland and Evan Harrel, my generous compassion teachers and friends: without you, this book would miss the point.
- Belinda, Nikita and Valérie, my compassion siblings and readers: without you, this book would be a lesser version of itself.
- My extraordinary, outstanding, compassionate product safety team: without you, this book could not redefine "success" as "what it takes to be yourself".
- All my other dear colleagues (you are recognizing yourselves, aren't you?), who have opened their heart to compassion in so many different ways: without you, my motto "never say no to compassion" would have remained an empty sentence.
- WIL-Europe, the amazing European Network for Women in Leadership that I serve as a volunteer: without you, my Applied Compassion Training Capstone Project would have been completely different.
- And my lovely cat Fuji, the best representative I could find of all those I wish to thank from the bottom of my heart for having contributed to my writing this book, even though they may never realize it.

Recommended Resources (my way too)

All along my journey, I have been discovering resources (most of which freely available on the net) that have provided me support, teachings, tools, comfort, enlightenment, or solace. Hopefully they will help you too!

Below, I will first list general references that address many of the topics and themes I have touched upon in my book, then more targeted articles, books, podcasts, and websites based on my own Alphabet of Compassion.

Enjoy and feel free to add your own preferred topics and resources!

Science-based Resources on Compassion

- https://www.globalcompassioncoalition.org/:
  a very complete website including blogposts, podcasts, and webinars (both recorded and upcoming), latest research, practices, and the possibility to connect with the global community of people interested in compassion.

- https://ccare.stanford.edu/:

  my second Alma Mater could not possibly be absent from my list of general resources about compassion—take a moment and explore its varied offer of scientific research, videos, podcasts, and blog posts about the different aspects of compassion.

- https://www.compassionatewellbeing.com/compassion-safe-relating-and-world-change-lecture-series.html:

  a series of foundational videos by Prof. Paul Gilbert on the science of compassion.

- https://www.mybestself101.org/:

  an attractive website launched and maintained by Jared Warren, PhD, an associate professor at Brigham Young University (Utah), and his young and dynamic research team. This website offers a wealth of modules to practice and reflect on many of the topics that run across the book, including flourishing, well-being, purpose, gratitude, happiness, etc.

- https://www.mindandlife.org/insight/the-science-of-compassion/:

  a very insightful summary article and video that you can use as a first shortcut to approach the science of compassion.

Compassion Resources: My A–Z

A

Acceptance:

   https://drdavidhamilton.com/the-power-of-acceptance-its-not-about-giving-up/.

Awe:

https://pmc.ncbi.nlm.nih.gov/articles/PMC10018061/.

B

Beauty:

Leading beautifully: How mastery, congruence and purpose create the aesthetic of embodied leadership practice.

C

Courage:

https://positivepsychology.com/courage/.

Curiosity:

https://greatergood.berkeley.edu/article/item/how_curiosity_can_help_us_overcome_disconnection - thank-influence.

D

Discernment:

https://www.psychologytoday.com/us/blog/social-lights/202404/cultivating-discernment.

E

Empathy:

https://www.sciencedirect.com/science/article/pii/S0960982214007702.

Equanimity:

https://positivepsychology.com/equanimity/.

F

Failure:

https://www.goodlifeproject.com/podcast/the-science-of-failing-well-amy-edmondson/.

Forgiveness:

https://www.thevirtualsanctuary.live/spiritual-teachings.

Freedom:

https://www.psychologytoday.com/us/blog/relationships-healing-relationships/202503/freedom-and-the-burden-of-empathy.

G

Goodness:

https://positiveorgs.bus.umich.edu/videos/hope-for-cynics-the-surprising-science-of-human-goodness/.

Gratitude:

https://rickhanson.com/practicing-gratitude/.

H

Happiness:

https://www.harvardmagazine.com/2007/01/the-science-of-happiness-html.

Hope:

https://theconversation.com/hope-brings-happiness-builds-grit-and-gives-life-meaning-heres-how-to-cultivate-it-218838.

I

Intention:

https://www.unity.org/article/compassion-why-it-matters-healing. This article describes a very interesting scientific experiment on the power of compassionate intentions toward people we feel an empathic bond with, even when they do not know we are sending good wishes to them. My favorite quote: "We are at a landmark moment in Western medicine in which compassion and empathy are being recognized as a complement to material interventions such as pharmaceuticals and surgical procedures. The result is a form of healing that is more effective than when either approach is used alone."

Introspection:

https://positivepsychology.com/introspection-self-reflection/.

J

Joy:

The Book of Joy—Lasting Happiness in a Changing World, His Holiness the Dalai Lama and Archbishop Desmond Tutu.

K

Kindness:

https://greatergood.berkeley.edu/article/item/world_happiness_report_highlights_everyday_kindness.

L

(Compassionate) Leadership:

My reference website is: https://www.centerforcompassionateleadership.org/.

You may also want to check out this webinar organized by the Global Compassion Coalition in 2024, "How do we get the leaders we want?": https://www.youtube.com/watch?v=HoYo9aVS_Go.

Letting go:

https://rickhanson.com/train-brain-letting-go-2/.

M

Meditation apps (free versions available):

Insight Timer, Healthy Minds.

Mindfulness:

Tarah Brach and Jack Kornfield generously offer their "Mindfulness daily" course for free here:

https://courses.tarabrach.com/courses/mindfulness-daily.

And for those who wish to take a step further, here comes the free version of the Mindfulness-Based Stress Reduction (MBSR) course, based on the original MBSR curriculum developed by Jon Kabat-Zinn: https://palousemindfulness.com/MBSR/index.html.

Serge followed it and found it awesome!

Money:

A blog post titled "Money and Personal Growth: The Deep Connection", https://money-meets-life.com/money-personal/.

N

Neuroplasticity:

The science of how we can change ourselves by practicing compassion, forgiveness, mindfulness, etc.:

https://www.thinkingmatters.com/news/neuroplasticity-and-growth-mindset-whats-the-connection.

O

Openness:

https://medium.com/@joshua.wise/staying-open-to-compassion-even-when-you-cant-3618815b7376.

P

Purpose:

https://alumni.cornell.edu/cornellians/purpose-psychology/.

Q

Quietness:

https://medium.com/@maxkmurphy/the-gift-of-stillness-why-we-need-quietness-solitude-and-contemplation-a2ba18328162.

R

Routines:

https://greatergood.berkeley.edu/article/item/six_habits_of_highly_compassionate_people.

S

Self-compassion:

https://self-compassion.org/.

This is Kristin Neff's foundational website on self-compassion, offering numerous resources to understand the science behind self-compassion and practice it. You can even test your level of self-compassion to uncover your personal baseline!

Surrender:

https://www.susanchoiwellness.com/compassion-as-an-aspect-of-surrender/.

T

Trauma:

https://www.meditatehappier.com/meditationblog/caring-for-trauma-with-compassion.

U

Unconditional love:

https://www.psychologytoday.com/intl/blog/peaceful-parents-happy-kids/201307/giving-unconditional-love-when-you-didnt-get-it-yourself.

V

Vulnerability:

Brené Brown's hypnotic TED Talk "The Power of Vulnerability": https://www.youtube.com/watch?v=iCvmsMzlF7o.

W

Well-being:

> https://centerhealthyminds.org/join-the-movement/%E2%80%8B why-well-being-is-skill.

Window of Tolerance:

> Dan Siegel coined this expression in 1999, and it has taken some time for me to understand the great importance of this concept in expanding our growth. Hopefully the following articles will help you too: https://www.nicabm.com/trauma-how-to-help-your-clients-understand-their-window-of-tolerance/;
>
> https://www.psychologytoday.com/intl/blog/making-the-whole-beautiful/202205/what-is-the-window-of-tolerance-and-why-is-it-so-important;
>
> https://positivepsychology.com/window-of-tolerance/.

Wisdom:

> https://www.psychologytoday.com/us/basics/wisdom.

X

Well, I haven't found it yet, can you help me here?

Y

Yes, and:

> The improvisational theater rule that can be practiced in everyday life to increase openness, acceptance and creativity: https://www.amindapart.org.uk/blog/the-real-meaning-of-the-improv-rule-yes-and/.

Z

Zen:

https://thichnhathanhfoundation.org/about-us.

The Book Playlist

If you would like to listen to the playlist of the book on Spotify, here is the link: https://open.spotify.com/playlist/4TdBFmXKO8J1fOUqW7SjTM.

Movies and Series

I have also put together a viewing list of movies (+ a couple of series) I would recommend wholeheartedly, not only because they are really good, but also because the story they tell is infused with compassion, self-compassion, compassionate leadership, or one or more of the pillars of compassion. Whether you pick one that inspires you or whether you watch them all, I promise you will not be disappointed. I have simply sorted them by genre and alphabetical order to help you navigate through this long list:

Action movies
- *Hunter Killer*, Donovan Marsh, 2018.

- *Rebel Ridge*, Jeremy Saulnier, 2024.
- *Unforgiven*, Clint Eastwood, 1992.

Animated movies

- *Flow*, Gints Zilbalodis, 2023.
- *Inside Out*, Pete Docter, 2015.
- *Inside Out 2*, Kelsey Mann, 2024.

Comedy movies

- *Campeones*, Javier Fesser, 2018.
- *C.O.D.A.*, Sian Heder, 2021.
- *Dr. Strangelove*, Stanley Kubrick, 1964.
- *Hors normes*, Olivier Nakache & Éric Toledano, 2019.
- *It's a Wonderful Life*, Frank Capra, 1946.
- *Les intouchables*, Olivier Nakache & Éric Toledano, 2011.
- *Modern Times*, Charlie Chaplin, 1936.
- *Next Goal Wins*, Taika Waititi, 2023.
- *Ténor*, Claude Zidi Jr., 2022.

Drama

- *Adolescence* (series), Philip Barantini, 2025.
- *A Hidden Life*, Terrence Malick, 2019.
- *Mr Bates vs The Post Office* (series), 2024.
- *All About Eve*, Joseph L. Mankiewicz, 1950.
- *Andrei Roublev*, Andrei Tarkovski, 1966.
- *Armageddon Times*, James Gray, 2022.

- *Crash*, Paul Haggis, 2004.
- *Dead Man Walking*, Tim Robbins, 1995.
- *Gran Torino*, Clint Eastwood, 2008.
- *Il Vangelo secondo Matteo*, Pier Paolo Pasolini, 1964.
- *Incendies*, Denis Villeneuve, 2010.
- *Ladri di biciclette*, Vittorio De Sica, 1948.
- *La vita è bella*, Roberto Benigni, 1997.
- *Le Fils*, Frères Dardenne, 2002.
- *One Flew Over the Cuckoo's Nest*, Miloš Forman, 1975.
- *Radical*, Christopher Zalla, 2023.
- *Red Beard*, Akira Kurosawa, 1965.
- *Rocco e i suoi fratelli*, Luchino Visconti, 1960.
- *Schindler's List*, Steven Spielberg, 1993.
- *The Decalogue* (series), Krzysztof Kieślowski, 1989.
- *The Shawshank Redemption*, Frank Darabont, 1994.
- *Todo sobre mi madre*, Pedro Almodóvar, 1999.
- *To Kill a Mockingbird*, Robert Mulligan, 1962.
- *Va, vis et deviens*, Radu Mihaileanu, 2005.

Science Fiction

- *Metropolis*, Fritz Lang, 1927.
- *The Matrix*, The Wachowskis, 1999.
- *The Matrix Reloaded*, The Wachowskis, 2003.
- *The Matrix Revolutions*, The Wachowskis, 2003.

What It Takes to Be Yourself

You can add below your own selection (don't hesitate to share with me on LinkedIn: https://www.linkedin.com/in/pinuccia-contino/).

www.ingramcontent.com/pod-product-compliance
Lightning Source LLC
Chambersburg PA
CBHW021142160426
43194CB00007B/660